The Last Days of Empire and the Worlds of Business and Diplomacy

The Last Days of Empire and the Worlds of Business and Diplomacy

An Inside Account

Charles Cullimore

PEN & SWORD
HISTORY

First published in Great Britain in 2021 by
Pen & Sword History
An imprint of
Pen & Sword Books Ltd
Yorkshire – Philadelphia

ISBN 978 1 52678 904 4

Typeset by Mac Style
Printed and bound in the UK by TJ Books Ltd,
Padstow, Cornwall.

MIX
Paper from
responsible sources
FSC® C013056

Pen & Sword Books Limited incorporates the imprints of Atlas,
Archaeology, Aviation, Discovery, Family History, Fiction, History,
Maritime, Military, Military Classics, Politics, Select, Transport,
True Crime, Air World, Frontline Publishing, Leo Cooper, Remember
When, Seaforth Publishing, The Praetorian Press, Wharncliffe
Local History, Wharncliffe Transport, Wharncliffe True Crime
and White Owl.

For a complete list of Pen & Sword titles please contact

PEN & SWORD BOOKS LIMITED
47 Church Street, Barnsley, South Yorkshire, S70 2AS, England
E-mail: enquiries@pen-and-sword.co.uk
Website: www.pen-and-sword.co.uk

Or

PEN AND SWORD BOOKS
1950 Lawrence Rd, Havertown, PA 19083, USA
E-mail: Uspen-and-sword@casematepublishers.com
Website: www.penandswordbooks.com

To Val

Contents

Preface

The text which follows was essentially written as a memoir. My chosen title was 'Temporary Person Passing Through'. I believe this was the wording of the stamp put into the passports of visitors to India in the nineteen sixties. It also sums up the gypsy existence led by my wife, our children and me over a major part of our lives. Beyond that it of course describes the human condition of all of us. However my publishers have decided that the book may also be of interest to academics and students of history, hence the title.

In any case it is an attempt to recount and describe the nature of the life led by my family and me through successive incarnations in Her Majesty's Overseas Civil Service, ICI, and the Diplomatic Service over a total period of thirty-six years. From the time when Val and I met at Oxford our journey was all along a joint enterprise. It involved a good deal of hard work, and some hardship and disruption of family life. But it was also a lot of fun. I could not have done any of it without Val's constant help and support.

As I never kept a diary, the resulting text is an attempt to capture my recollections of a long, varied and lucky life in a range of very different countries at a time of rapid change from the end of Empire to our decision to leave the European Union. I hope that the reader will find the book at times entertaining and informative. It is not intended to be controversial. However on the evidence of my first hand experience at the grass roots level in Tanganyika in the final years before independence I hope that it will help to counter the widespread myth about the so-called evils of the British Empire, especially in its twilight era.

Apart from Bonn at the height of the Cold War all of our overseas postings were in Commonwealth countries. Of these India was the most fascinating. But I started in Africa and it is with the African continent that I have remained most engaged since retiring from the Diplomatic Service.

Acknowledgments

I would like to thank everyone who has helped and encouraged me in writing this memoir. My particular thanks are due to Lester Crook, initially as a source of encouragement after he had seen the very first incomplete text, and more recently as editor. I am also greatly indebted to Lord Luce for his introduction which goes way beyond anything the book deserves. My dear friend and former editor of the Folio Society, Sue Whitley, has been most helpful with her comments and practical suggestions, as has Hubert Schaafsma who is a good friend and is himself a former publisher.

I would also like to thank my daughter Fiona and grandchildren Jenny and Tom for their interest and helpfulness. Finally I thank Val for her patient understanding and forbearance and helpful correction of various infelicities. Even though the book is partly about the key role she has played in it all she has never sought to make any changes of substance.

Charles Cullimore
Bidborough, Kent.

Introduction

by The Rt Hon the Lord Luce KG GCVO

Memoirs are always valuable to our families and friends. Charles Cullimore's autobiography should be read far more widely. It is a compelling description of a thoroughly varied life covering post-war years and is valuable historically.

It strikes a chord with me immediately for we were both amongst a small privileged group who, following National Service, studied at Oxbridge and started our careers as the last District Officers in the twilight of the Empire. This was preceded by an extra year at Oxford to complete a demanding and varied course to join Her Majesty's Overseas Civil Service. In both our experiences we only had a chance to serve two or three years before Tanganyika (now Tanzania), and in my case Kenya, became independent. But the experience deeply affected the rest of our lives.

Charles's description of his life and responsibilities as a district officer should be read by anyone who is interested in the history of the British Empire. The title of his book is an accurate description of his life and of many of us in those times. What is striking is that most of us who served as colonial administrators regarded it as the greatest possible privilege. Indeed the inscription on the memorial plaque to Her Majesty's Overseas Civil Service in Westminster Abbey's Cloisters reads 'Whosoever be chief among you let him be your servant.'

Remaining survivors from those earlier times have a duty to put a perspective on why it was a privilege to serve people in all countries of the globe in an empire which has long since gone. Perhaps it is best summed up in the personal message from President Nyerere to Charles and all those serving in Tanganyika inviting British administrators to stay on after independence. If anything, that was testimony to the goodwill which

Overseas Civil Servants generated in countries that they were lucky enough to serve in.

The next interesting question is what did all those young administrators go on to do in life? In Charles's case his earlier experiences showed through in all the subsequent jobs, firstly in ICI as a personnel manager where he served in Scotland, London, Brussels and, interestingly, Malaysia, where he obviously felt at home. Then followed twenty-three years of distinguished service in the Diplomatic Service ranging from senior posts in Germany, India, Australia and London. His career culminated most appropriately in Uganda. As High Commissioner he witnessed the early years of President Museveni, when he was struggling to stabilise the country and to restore order and unity after the devastating years of Amin and later Obote. His description of this period is important historically but also brings out the value of his experiences as a district officer as he got to know all parts of the country. In the same way he made absolutely sure that he got to know Australia and India well, travelling to all quarters of those countries.

Charles's description of all his experiences is colourful, full of humorous as well as serious stories of the many people he met over a very full life.

Throughout the book it becomes clear that his wife Val has been not only an immense support to him but has been vigorously active in her charitable and other tasks that she took on voluntarily. It has been a splendid partnership.

After leaving the Diplomatic Service Charles remained very active in tasks wholly relevant to his career including being Chief Executive of the Southern Africa Business Association. He ended up as the last Chairman of the Overseas Civil Service Pensioners' Association where he was able to do his best to ensure that the legacy of our Empire is understood and kept in perspective in a very different age.

It is a pleasure to recommend this story of a richly varied and interesting life.

Chapter 1

Early Life in Ulster

I grew up in a rambling old Rectory at the top of a hill in Omagh opposite the large grey neo-Gothic pile of St Columba's parish church of which my father was the rector. Behind the house on a west-facing slope was an overgrown Victorian garden of fruit trees, shrubberies, and flower beds. There was also an assortment of out-buildings on three sides of a large yard which at various times housed chickens, a goat optimistically christened Buttercup by my mother though it never produced any milk, the winter's supply of turf, and my father's Morris10 car. Pride of the garden had been a large, dilapidated hot-house with huge rusting iron pipes and a rambling vine which still managed to produce an abundance of grapes each year. With its old iron flue serving as a periscope it doubled as a make believe submarine where my friends and I could play our wartime games.

I had no brothers or sisters but I did have an irascible Irish terrier, inevitably called Paddy, whom I loved dearly. There were also two resident cats – Mina (because she was mine) and Pinkle Purr. Paddy had an implacable foe, a large white-haired mongrel with a marbled eye. On many occasions I had to haul Paddy away from attacking him. When they did fight the contest was hopelessly one-sided but Paddy never seemed to learn. Victor, the mongrel, belonged to the church sexton – a formidable Boer war veteran with a waxed black moustache.

My father was a saintly man but not very practical, the last of which traits I share though sadly not the first. As the Church of Ireland rector he was unavoidably part of the Protestant establishment. But he abhorred bigotry and did his best to ignore the sectarian divide which then, as now, ran through the town. He often met the priest in charge of the huge Roman Catholic church with its soaring twin spires just down the hill from the Rectory. Probably neither the priest's flock nor my father's would have approved of these meetings. During the war my father organised ecumenical services in the local cinema on a Sunday night for the troops of all denominations, and none, from the Infantry Training Centre on the edge of town. The cinema was always packed even though attendance was entirely voluntary, unlike the compulsory church parades on Sunday mornings to St. Columba's. In contrast to many of his fellow clergy he had nothing to do with the Orange Order and, as far as I know, never attended their parades. In short he was well ahead of his time for a Protestant churchman in Northern Ireland.

I should add that he was also devoted to his parishioners, and much loved by them. On week days we hardly saw him during the day as he was usually away visiting the sick either in hospital or in their own homes. I now realise that in those days priests and clergy had a vital role in ministering to sick and depressed people. There were, of course, no social services and no such thing as professional carers. He was also much involved in numerous committees and local organizations.

The Rectory stood opposite the church and at the top of a steep street of mean houses lived in by poor Catholic families. Unimaginable today, there was no running water in the houses and the whole street depended on a single standpipe for its water where the women collected it in buckets and pails. Typically my father had no objection to my playing in the back garden of the Rectory with Catholic boys of my own age from the street and from the nearby housing estate graphically known as Gallows Hill. If they had known many of his parishioners would not have been amused. I was also often sent to buy milk and bread from a little Catholic grocery shop at the bottom of the street. I took all this for granted at the time and only later came to realise that such behaviour was quite unusual. Protestants normally only bought from Protestant shops, and Protestant and Catholic children did not mix.

My father could scarcely have imagined that 'our wee town' would one day be the scene of the worst single atrocity in the entire IRA bombing campaign some forty years later.

He had grown up in a modest semi-detached house in Rathmines, South Dublin, where he was one of six children, four boys and two girls. He was the only one of his siblings who ever married. Although the family were not well off, he managed to get himself through Trinity College, Dublin, paying for his studies by working as a clerk on the Great Northern Railway (Ireland) which ran trains from Dublin to Belfast and from Belfast to Derry via Omagh. From TCD, with an MA in Divinity, he went into the church and was for several years a curate in a busy Anglican parish in south London before becoming Rector of Raphoe in what was then thought of as the wilds of Donegal. While there, at the height of the earlier Irish 'troubles', he had several encounters with the notorious Black and Tans. On one occasion he flatly refused to allow them to mount a machine gun on the square tower of the little cathedral church. On another he risked arrest at a Black and Tan checkpoint by telling the officer in charge of the checkpoint, when asked if he had anything to declare, that he had five revolvers. As they became rather agitated at this revelation he explained that he was referring to the four wheels on the car and the spare, or stepney as it used to be called. They were not amused.

In due course, after a spell in the suburban parish of Glendermott outside Derry, he became Rector of St Columba's in Omagh with Mountfield, and a Canon of St Patrick's cathedral in Dublin. He was an eloquent preacher and a considerable theologian.

I only once saw my father lose his cool. This was during a 'junior church' service as we used to call them – a kind of mix of bible class and Sunday school held in the church itself on Sunday afternoons. One of the children at the back of the church let out a shrill whistle which caused my father to demand in a resounding voice 'who dared to whistle in the house of God?' The only answer was a stunned silence but the rest of the service was conducted with due reverence and I never heard another whistle. Towards me he was far too indulgent which left my mother having to impose such discipline as there was, i.e. not very much.

My mother was partly English (a fact of which she never ceased to remind us) and an evangelical Christian ever since she had attended one of the famous Keswick Conventions. She was also an accomplished pianist and painter in water colours. She carried out the duties of a parson's wife with enthusiasm and panache whether running the Mother's Union or organising meetings of the Girls Friendly Society who, much to my delight, came to the Rectory every Saturday morning to sing choruses. My mother had suffered a severe Victorian up-bringing as a child at the hands of her step-grandmother, and also her step-mother, with whom she had been parked at an early age after her mother had died in India aged barely twenty-one. She saw little of her father who was a Colonel in the Indian army having transferred from the Royal Dublin Fusiliers. He was killed trying to lift the Turkish siege at Kut Al Amara in Mesopotamia, now Iraq, in the First World War.

My mother was immensely proud of her descent, on her mother's side, from the Gilbert family and thereby from Sir Humphrey Gilbert and Sir Walter Raleigh. Her great ambition was for me to join the navy and go to sea, in the tradition of the Gilbert family, via Dartmouth. Fortunately for me, and for the navy, this was ruled out early on by my poor eyesight. Perhaps because I was an only child, and as a reaction to her own very strict upbringing, I was allowed a virtually free rein to come and go as I pleased and to roam about the town.

Living in a remote part of north-west Ireland, the war years affected us remarkably little. The main impact was that the town was full of soldiers. In the first three years they came from a succession of British army regiments stationed at the Infantry Training Centre at Lisanelly camp. Later in the run up to D-day they were joined by large numbers of American GIs who were billeted all over the place including in the Church Hall next door to the Rectory. Consequently our house became a kind of home from home for many GIs and for officers and men from the ITC including on one occasion both Hedley Verity and Norman Yardley who were stationed in Omagh with the Green Howards. Verity was later killed in Sicily, but Yardley went on after the war to be vice captain and then captain of England. I cheekily wrote to him when he was in Australia with the first MCC side to tour after the war led by Wally Hammond. To my great joy he wrote back with the autographs of all the England team including the great Wally Hammond himself, Len Hutton and Denis Compton, who was my boyhood hero. My father was a keen follower of the game. One of his favourite stories was of how he had seen Jessop, of Gloucester and England, hit a six from College Green in Dublin clean through a window of the Kildare Street Club, well beyond the college grounds.

I would occasionally accompany him on his parish rounds to visit the sick or parishioners with other problems. On such visits I would sometimes be invited into the living room for a welcome mug of 'tay'. This would often be when my Dad was visiting in the remote parish of Mountfield in the foothills of the Sperrin mountains some seven miles from Omagh. Mountfield was a small farming community of old stone cottages with thatched roofs. The 'living room' was often the only room in the house. It had maybe a table and a few wooden chairs on a rough stone floor and always a turf fire burning in an open hearth with a black kettle hanging from a hook above the fire. Outside there would be a cow or two and a few chickens. Once or twice

I also went with him to select a turf stack from the nearby turf bogs. This would provide fuel for the Rectory fires to see us through the winter. The outing was a major annual event as it was important to ensure that the turf was of good quality and reasonably dry, at least in the middle of the stack. Once selected the turf would be delivered by a large, high-sided lorry into a turf shed behind the Rectory.

There was rationing of a sort and I think I saw my first banana when I was thirteen or fourteen. The blackout was however quite strict, and many decorative iron railings disappeared to help the war effort. However, with typical bravura, my mother managed to persuade the local authorities that the Rectory railings, and those around the church, were somehow special and should be preserved. She also persuaded the Home Guard that they should not use the ornamental aperture in our garden wall, which overlooked one of the main roads into town, to site a bren gun during their exercises. The reason for denying them this vantage point was that the bren gunner would have had to sit on her white arabis of which she was inordinately proud.

Eventually, aged ten, I was sent off to Rockport Preparatory school beautifully situated on the shores of Belfast Lough. Not before time. I had by then a number of chums from Omagh Academy, which I attended for two years, with whom various exploits were undertaken. I never really engaged with the school itself which seemed to me to be rather alien. I do recall that I had a particular problem with maths where I encountered algebra for the first time. I had somehow got the impression that every letter in the alphabet had a fixed value and that all would be revealed if only I could discover what those values were.

However our exploits out of school were many and varied. One popular pastime was shooting pellets at cows with my Diana air rifle which caused them to jump into the air in, to our eyes, a highly comical fashion. I believe the occasional pellet did no lasting harm though it may not have been good for the milk yield. We also tried our hand at making gunpowder in the backyard with saltpetre, black powder and sugar. In those days the hardest ingredient to obtain was sugar because it was rationed.

On another occasion a couple of us managed to find our way into a converted barn in the middle of town where a number of Bren gun carriers were parked, presumably having been allocated to the Home Guard. At any rate they were unattended so we climbed into one and to our great delight managed to start it before we were intercepted and sent packing. So much for security at the height of the war!

My proudest achievement was on a snowy day in winter when I knocked off the peak cap of a young RUC policeman with a snowball. Fortunately he saw the joke and we subsequently became good friends – a friendship which lasted a lifetime and in later life has led to our spending many a happy holiday in his partially converted boat house on the wild and beautiful Atlantic coast of Donegal. I say partially converted because it was, and still is, necessary to remove the boat in order to get in.

The area is still overwhelmingly Catholic and many folk also have Gaelic as their mother tongue. Yet when the tiny Church of Ireland church in nearby Dungloe was in urgent need of repair much of the cost was met by the surrounding Catholic parishes. Why do stories such as this never get into the press?

At Rockport I encountered serious discipline for the first time in my life but also discovered that I enjoyed learning. I was therefore in continuous competition with my peers to be top of the class. The Headmaster, Geoffrey Bing, who had founded the school before the First World War, was a stern but genial disciplinarian. He was an imposing figure with great black bushy eyebrows and a heavy walking stick which he wielded with frightening effect when roused. This was long before any notions of health and safety, still less of children's rights.

The war was still on and there was a constant procession of warships and Liberty ships in the Lough which were a source of great interest. Even more interestingly for us schoolboys there was a Luftwaffe prisoner of war camp in the field next to the school grounds. Thus many a half-holiday was spent happily trading our sweet ration through the barbed wire fence in exchange for German badges and insignia. This was all carried on under the benevolent eye of the camp guards though I doubt whether the school ever knew about it.

From Rockport I won a scholarship to Portora Royal School in Enniskillen which in those days was a leading all-Ireland school. It is probably the best known of the five royal schools founded by King James the First in 1608, and numbers among its past pupils both Oscar Wilde and Samuel Becket as well as Henry Francis Lyte the great hymn writer and author of 'Abide with Me'. The scholarship must have come as a welcome relief to my parents who were finding it quite hard to make ends meet on a Church of Ireland parson's meagre stipend. They never bought any clothes for themselves and even after the war we never ate out. The one luxury we had was an annual summer holiday either spent in a seaside boarding house in Portrush on the beautiful north Antrim coast, or occasionally in a country rectory near Dublin where my father would act as 'locum' for the regular rector. Although the war was still raging we hardly noticed it. In Portrush we had fun watching Spitfires carrying out target practice out at sea. In Dublin the main difference I remember was that cars and taxis were driving around with enormous gas bags on their roofs as there was very little petrol. However Belfast was heavily bombed on several nights in 1941 and large fires were started. In an early example of cross border cooperation Dublin's fire engines were rushed over the border to Belfast to help put out the flames.

After the war, in the glorious summer of '47, we had the gorgeous Georgian Rectory at Dalkey complete with tennis court and within five minutes bicycle ride of the famous '40 foot' men only bathing pool in the rocks opposite Dalkey Island where skinny dipping, as it would now be called, was the norm. It was also close to the Martello Tower made famous by James Joyce. If it still exists the Rectory would be worth millions today.

At about this time I also had the annual excitement of being sent on summer camps under the aegis of an organisation called Varsity and Public Schools Camps (known as Veeps for short). The first was in the Glenmalure valley in the Wicklow mountains, and the second was near the coast in Co Wexford. There were about forty boys from a variety of boarding schools mainly in southern Ireland. The camps were inspired and run by a commandant (commie for short), the Reverend E M Neill, who was an evangelical Church of Ireland clergyman. We slept on palliases, hessian bags stuffed with straw, in seven-man bell tents, and cooked mainly on open fires. When not busy on camp chores we climbed the nearby hills including Ireland's second highest, Lugnaquilla, or swam in the river or the nearby lake. At the Wexford camp we swam in the sea. The camps were a kind of microcosm of open air, muscular Christianity with daily prayers in a central marquee.

My life changed for ever at fifteen when my parents died within two months of each other. But I was extremely lucky in having my mother's half-brother as my guardian, and a very supportive Headmaster at Portora, the Reverend Douglas Graham. He even offered to let me bring the only other survivor of the family, Paddy the Irish terrier, back to school with me after my mother's funeral – an offer which I sensibly declined. My uncle had already had a distinguished career in the Indian army before independence having fought the Italians in Abyssinia, the Germans in North Africa and the Japanese in Assam and Burma. In his early thirties during the Burma campaign he became the youngest brigadier in the Indian army. When I asked him years later how this had come about his laconic reply, typical of his generation, was ' the brigadier was shaving one morning and he got shot, so I took over'. Nothing more to be said.

By the time my parents died (in November 1948 and January 1949) Uncle Harry had transferred to the British army and was posted to Malaya, as it then was. Later, when he and his wife and family were back in the UK they generously offered me a home from home during school holidays and beyond. It says much about my mother's attitude to life that several years earlier, during the battle of El Alamein, in which he was in the thick of things with the 4th Indian Division, my uncle received a letter from her asking if he would take care of me if anything should happen to my father and to her. He told me years later that the letter had done wonders for his morale! It was also my good fortune that the family of the policeman who had befriended me in Omagh took me into their home in Enniskillen for many a happy holiday. I owe them a debt of gratitude which I shall never be able to repay. With support like this, although I had lost my parents at an early age,and had no siblings, I came to look upon the world as a friendly oyster.

Portora at that time was dominated by the said headmaster, a commanding figure in his long black cassock and white bow tie. He was a classics scholar, had taught at Eton, and been a chaplain in the Royal Navy during the war. His wartime service included sailing to Murmansk on a cruiser escorting the Arctic convoys and being torpedoed. He had also been a keen boxer in his day and a front row forward for Trinity College, Dublin where he was chosen to play in a final trial for the Irish XV. The story was that the selectors eventually passed him over because his style of play was considered to be too 'robust'.

The school also had a number of talented and dedicated staff to whom many of us pupils owe a great deal. One who stands out still was the diminutive George Andrews, inevitably known as 'titch'. With a degree in French from Cambridge he had served as a liaison officer in the Free French navy during the war. He had been awarded the Croix de Guerre for his actions in saving a French destroyer which had been damaged by German shellfire in the Mediterranean. Apparently nearly all the French officers, including the captain, had been killed or injured when a shell struck the bridge. So George, who was unhurt, simply took over the ship and got it back safely to port.

He was way ahead of his time in his teaching methods in which spoken French was the language in the classroom from day one. If you tried to speak English you were just ignored. This early familiarity with spoken French coupled with frequent visits to Lausanne, where my godmother lived, and to France was to prove particularly useful for me in later years in the Diplomatic Service. George was also instrumental in developing Portora into the leading rowing school in Ireland and producing several eights which competed at Henley. As a keen cricketer I never rowed but we were all proud of the achievements of the rowing club. Another important out of school activity was the Combined Cadet Force (CCF) which boasted a pipe band and a splendid 25-pounder gun. The latter was a cause of acute embarrassment one day when on the occasion of an inspection by a senior army officer we managed to get a long-handled broom, which we had been using to clean it, stuck in the barrel. For some reason our commanding officer 'Buddy' Halpin, a Dubliner with a distinguished war record, decided to make me Company Sergeant Major of the Corps in my last year. I enjoyed the privilege though I never felt cut out to be a soldier.

The ethos of the school was broad Church of Ireland rather than narrowly Protestant. More than half of the boarders came from the south of Ireland. There were also several boys who came over from Scotland and England, and one or two from further afield including the son of a former Mayor of Warsaw who at the age of fifteen had fought against and escaped from the Nazis. Typically it was George Andrews who had taken him under his wing at the end of the war and got him into Portora.

Discipline was firm but not oppressive. The main punishments were detention and, for the boarders, 'gating'. In the days of post war rationing food was pretty basic and had to be supplemented by supplies from home or, as many of us did, by cycling across the border into the Republic, eleven miles away, and returning with saddle-bags stuffed with goodies unobtainable or strictly rationed in Northern Ireland such as bananas, chocolate and creamery butter. The customs authorities at the border indulgently chose to turn a blind eye to these schoolboy smugglers.

Had the liberal Church of Ireland ethos been more widespread I believe that Ulster might have been spared the violence which has scarred a generation. But this was never on the cards. The Church was still seen as the embodiment of a privileged class and had little appeal either to the under-privileged Catholic minority or to the largely Presbyterian working class in Belfast.

In the event, partly as a result of the troubles, the school ceased some years ago to be a boarding school and hence is no longer the all-Ireland school which it once was. In effect it reverted to its original role as a boys' grammar school for County Fermanagh. More recently still it has been merged with the Collegiate Girls School in Enniskillen (a long overdue merger) and both schools have acquired a new name, Enniskillen Royal Grammar School.

Happily the cross-border connection lives on through a link with Clongowes Wood Jesuit College near Dublin. This takes the form of an annual Joyce/Becket prize which alternates between the two schools. In one year Clongowes awards the prize for the best essay on Joyce by a pupil at Portora and the following year it is the turn of Portora to award the prize for the best essay on Becket by a pupil at Clongowes. (Joyce was a pupil at Clongowes and Becket at Portora). Accordingly the two schools play host to each other in alternate years.

I left Portora early at the end of the spring term in 1952 and took a temporary job for the summer term at a somewhat eccentric preparatory school on the beautiful shore of Lake Windermere near Ambleside. The school was run by the brother of one of the housemasters at Portora, Major Butler, who arranged the appointment for me. It catered mainly for the sons of wealthy industrialists from Manchester and Liverpool. For reasons best known to the Headmaster, the ethos of the school was based around the morality of the Knights of the Round Table. The head himself was a somewhat remote figure with whom one was supposed to communicate by leaving notes in pre-arranged places. Not surprisingly the 'places' were discovered by the boys which meant that they had great fun reading them.

I found myself teaching a variety of subjects including Maths which was not exactly my forte. I also had to devise a form of cricket which could be played on the tennis court as there was no cricket pitch. Together with another teacher we were accommodated in the gate lodge to the school which had the added advantage of being next door to a well known pub, "The Drunken Duckling". The pub boasted one of the few television sets around in 1952 where we were able to watch part of the test series against Australia.

Chapter 2

Oxford

It was the norm for boys from Portora to go on either to Trinity College Dublin or Queens University Belfast, or to Sandhurst. However, with much encouragement from Douglas Graham, and the indulgence of its Senior Tutor, the redoubtable Michael Maclagan, I found myself at Trinity College, Oxford where a whole new world opened up. I set out to make the most of it. As a result I ended up doing many things though none of them particularly well.

In my first year I had rooms in the now iconic cottages on The Broad dating from the fourteenth century, though at the time I thought little of it. In truth the rooms were quite small and cramped. The study was on a slant to the left so that if you put a pencil on the desk it would simply roll off on to the floor and then roll further into a corner. One advantage however was that just below me on the ground floor was a room looking out on to the street. The window was barred but, unbeknownst to the college authorities, one of the bars was removable from the inside leaving just enough space for a reasonably slim person to slide through. This was a great asset in the days when gentlemen were required to be back in college by midnight. The occupant of the room in question, one Aldo Arpino was, needless to say, one of the most popular undergraduates in the college whose friendship was much sought after. In my second year I had the rare privilege of a room on a staircase whose occupants were looked after by the one and only Cadman, reputedly the doyen of all college scouts in the university at the time.

Until my last year I spent an inordinate amount of time acting both in University and college productions. The college had a very lively thespian group, the Trinity Players, which toured the West Country in July each year. We performed in a variety of schools or sometimes in a local theatre, usually camping in a nearby field. By way of contrast I also joined the University Officers Training Corps (OTC) which happened to be an artillery unit. Each summer, at Bulford camp on Salisbury Plain, we spent many thousands of pounds of taxpayers' money firing hundreds of shells from our twenty-five pounder guns. In the process we managed to kill a few unfortunate sheep. The main attraction however was that we were linked to an all female TA unit from London University who acted as observers or spotters for the gun crews. There was also one useful perk. Instead of my having to pay an instructor to teach me to drive, the army paid me to learn! The chosen vehicle was a heavy armoured 'quad' specially designed for towing field guns. I vividly recall having to change down through the gears with no syncromesh while driving down Headington Hill into Oxford. Fortunately I managed it without disaster. But it was certainly not a skill ever taught by the driving schools.

Apart from touring with the Trinity Players and some mild training with the OUTC, I also managed to earn a little extra money in the long summer vac by getting a temporary job as a steward on board Sealink's *Maid of Orleans* sailing between Folkestone and Boulogne. In addition we could earn a bit more by carrying bags for embarking and disembarking passsengers. During the actual crossing of the Channel I was first asked to take charge of making toast for breakfast in the main restaurant. This turned out to be not a good idea. After many hundreds of slices of bread were reduced to ashes it was recognised that trying to produce fifty slices of toast simultaneously without automatic toasters was not my forte. The management then discovered that I could speak French and I found myself promoted to wine waiter in the first class restaurant. That there was apparently no other French-speaking waiter on the ship routinely carrying hundreds of French passengers speaks for itself.

At one point I had been given a few hours of shore leave in France and decided to travel from Boulogne to Calais to explore. Unfortunately I did not know that the French Railways Union had just called a 24-hour strike so there were no trains back to Boulogne in time for me to catch the next sailing of the *Maid of Orleans*. Nor did I have enough money for a taxi and there did not seem to be a bus. What to do ? In the event I got chatting to an engine driver at Calais station who, as it happened, lived in Boulogne and had decided to drive his engine back there in order to get home. When I explained my predicament to him to my delight he invited me to join him on the footplate. So I not only got back to the ship in time but also fulfilled a boyhood dream. It is hard to imagine such a scenario in today's world.

After a belated spell of hard work in my final year I managed to emerge with a respectable second in Modern History. With hindsight this was mainly a tribute to the quality of my tutors, Michael Maclagan and John Cooper, who managed to be both easy-going and challenging, though totally different in character. Maclagan in particular, whose speciality was early English history, was a memorable figure. Tall and ramrod-straight, he could be a bit daunting at times but he and his wife were always kind and hospitable. He was also a Herald at Arms and, for a year, Mayor of Oxford.

As time goes by I have maintained my links with Trinity and am increasingly conscious of how lucky I was to spend my Oxford days there. While it was not among the most academic of colleges it nevertheless had an able Senior Common Room (the well known Norrington Table was the brainchild of the then President). At the same time there was a lively recognition of the value of extra mural activities. Trinity also probably had, and still has, the best food in Oxford and an excellent wine cellar.

Best of all, at Oxford I met and fell in love with my future wife, Val. She had come to Oxford to learn English after spending a year living with a French family and attending Nancy University from which she had a diploma in French literature. As it happened she was staying with a lady who was herself half French and consequently the language in the house was mainly French. So it was natural for us to speak French together, and it was several days before I discovered that Val, who spoke French fluently and with no accent, was in fact from just east of Berlin. The family had managed to escape to the West after the war. In any case for me it was love at first sight.

Val and her young brother had spent their early childhood with their parents in a small village near Königswusterhausen.. It is a beautiful area of lakes and woods south east of Berlin where the German army defending Berlin made its last stand at the end of the war. The Willemsen family were right in the middle of it. Her father had moved the family there before the war. He had been a legal adviser in the Post Office who, as an official, had been required to take an oath of allegiance to Hitler. With great courage he had refused to do this and was promptly sacked. Somehow he avoided any worse treatment and, even more amazingly, they all survived the mayhem at the end of the war. The story of how Val's father walked away from a blazing Berlin, where he had been drafted as part of the ragtag Volksturm to defend

Hitler's bunker, is legendary. However it belongs as part of another story about the survival of Val and her family.

On one occasion Val's mother came close to being shot by an SS officer who, in the midst of the Russian bombardment, wanted to take over their cellar where they were hiding some refugees, including, unbeknownst to the SS, a Jew who had been living in the village. When the officer asked her to evacuate the cellar she refused so he threatened to shoot her unless she complied. At this point miraculously she was saved by a bolt of lightning which came crashing down the steps and knocked the officer flat on the floor. After this the young SS men decided to leave. They were never seen again. A few days later, after the Russians had taken over, Val's family and the refugee family were ordered to leave the village along with many others. As their little group was trudging towards Berlin they were held up by a drunken Russian soldier who threatened to shoot them all. In the event their lives were saved by the same Jew they had been hiding from the SS. He had managed to obtain a laissez-passer from the Russian commandant in the village. When he produced this the soldier relented and waved them on.

With hindsight I now recognise that Val's father, Robert Willemsen, and her mother, Elizabeth, were two of the most courageous and remarkable people I ever had the privilege of knowing.

Chapter 3

The Army

After Oxford I obtained a Northern Ireland short service commission in the Royal Inniskilling Fusiliers, 'the Skins'. The name comes from Enniskillen where the regiment was raised at the time of the siege in 1689 by the forces of James the Second. Another regiment, the Royal Inniskilling Dragoon Guards, was also named after Enniskillen, which is the only town in the Commonwealth which can claim to have been the birthplace of two regiments Although there was no national service in Ulster I felt that everyone else in Britain had to do it and I did not want to feel like a second-class citizen in my own country. My officer training consisted of a sixteen-week intensive course at the requisitioned Eaton Hall, an imposing neo-Gothic house in many acres of parkland outside Chester which was part of the Duke of Westminster's estate.

One of my most enduring memories from my time there is of RSM Lynch of the Irish Guards who, with his commanding presence, powerful voice and rich Irish brogue, dominated our lives. It was he who greeted the new arrivals nervously assembled in the drill hall on their first evening. By way of welcome he announced 'gentlemen, there is just one thing you need to know about tis place and that is that when you are talkin' to me you will call me sor and when I am talkin' to you I will call you sor – and the only difference between us is that you mean it.' Eight weeks later our platoon managed to 'pass off' the square which brought with it a number of privileges. This caused a night of heavy celebration following which we assembled the next morning for inspection rather the worse for wear. Surveying the scene with a stern face but a twinkle in his eye RSM Lynch began the inspection by announcing 'Gentlemen, your eyes are like pee-holes in the snow.' No doubt this was a well rehearsed expression but memorable nevertheless.

Val and I wanted to get married but, in those days of deference, it was customary for a junior officer to seek the approval of the Commanding Officer of the regiment beforehand. However any qualms I might have had were immediately laid to rest by the CO of the first battalion of the Inniskillings, Colonel Maxwell, affectionately known by all as 'Smudger'. 'No problem at all', he said ' the battalion is just a bloody great marriage bureau'.

So in June 1956 Val and I were married in the Johannes Kirche, a beautiful Romanesque church on the right bank of the Rhine near her parents' house south of Koblenz. In July we moved into our first home, a tiny flat in Frome in Somerset as there was no army quarter available. The battalion had just been posted to the Army School of Infantry at Warminster as demonstration battalion for the British army. It has always puzzled me how it could ever have been chosen for such a high-profile role since it was an explosive mix of Southern Irish volunteers and mainly cockney national servicemen. It had a fine combat record and had recently been granted the freedom of Nairobi for its part in the fight against Mau Mau. But peacetime soldiering was not its forté. There were many hilarious moments during my year at Warminster. On one occasion when my platoon was supposed to be demonstrating fire orders to a group of senior officers from friendly countries the men suddenly embarked on an apparently impromptu rendering of Bill Haley's 'Rock around the Clock'.* I wished the ground could have swallowed me up but fortunately most of our visitors had the grace to see the joke. To the best of my recollection the battalion also registered sixty-seven court martials in one year which must have been a record for any unit of the British army in peacetime. Most of the offenders were Irish volunteers who had overstayed their leaves back home in the Republic.

In the summer of 1956 the 'make-believe' world of military exercises on Salisbury Plain suddenly became more real and intense when the Suez crisis erupted and the government decided to invade Egypt and occupy the canal zone. The battalion was placed on standby, ready to be sent at 24-hours notice to reinforce the troops on the ground. Accordingly the next few weeks were spent in preparing for war in the desert which mainly meant painting anything that moved yellow, and getting equipped with tropical kit. There were also a number of hastily arranged marriages. However, just before we were due to go the whole operation was called off and we spent the next

---

* Fire orders were based on the mnemonic GRIT standing for group, range, indication (using a clock face) and target (using a prominent feature nearby if possible eg a rock). Thus in this instance the order given was "no 1 section -- 200-- 8o'clock-- rock", at which point army drill was superseded by an outburst of rock music.

few weeks painting everything camouflage green again. I have no idea what happened to the various marriages.

Any possibility of making the army my career was laid to rest one fine day during an exercise on Dartmoor. Leading my platoon in an attack on a hill heavily defended by 'the enemy', I completely misread the map and managed to attack the wrong hill which was defended only by a few rather bewildered sheep. The men had a good laugh but my company commander was not amused.

Nevertheless I believe that my brief exposure to army life did me a power of good. It also helped later in life when my various postings in the Diplomatic Service brought me much into contact with members of all three armed services.

Chapter 4

Tanganyika and Colonial Service

Before leaving the army I had applied to the Colonial Office for an administrative post in Her Majesty's Overseas Civil Service as it then was. I had a fairly perfunctory interview at Great Smith Street. However, I do recall my interviewer being impressed by the fact that I had done a certain amount of acting at Oxford and commenting that it would come in very useful in my new role as a district officer in Africa. Only later did I come to realise what a prescient observation this was. Shortly afterwards I was told that I had been successful, and I found myself allocated to Tanganyika.

The posting was preceded by a year's training on the Devonshire A course at Oxford, based at Rhodes House. Thus I was once again back in familiar surroundings. The Oxford course was developed for cadets going to East Africa. Cambridge covered West Africa and I think London did the other colonies. There were eleven of us in the Tanganyika contingent on the course in 1957-8, all white even at that late stage, and mainly British, though there was one Canadian. Several of the group had spent part of their childhood in one or other of the colonies. The Ugandan contingent did, however, include two Ugandans both of whom later became prominent in Uganda. I believe there were rather more Africans on the Cambridge course.

The course covered a wide range of subjects from Law to Social Anthropology to Tropical Agriculture, Field Engineering, Local Government, and the History of the Empire. We also spent an entertaining day in a local magistrates court in the east end of London. The magistrate dealt with about sixty cases in an afternoon. He had clearly been provided with a crib sheet beforehand of each accused's criminal record. The first question was in most cases 'were you drunk?'. If the answer was, as it usually was, in the affirmative he would then impose a fine which clearly varied according to the number of previous occasions when the accused had been drunk and disorderly in public. How times have changed!

Most importantly we were also given a thorough grounding in Swahili, the lingua franca of the country and the language used on a daily basis by the district administration. As Tanganyika was held as a UN Trust Territory rather than a colony it was deemed right and proper to promote Swahili rather than English as the national language, and all district officers were required to pass a Higher Swahili examination before they could be considered for promotion. Ironically, after independence President Nyerere chose to criticise the colonial authorities for denying his people the benefit of English! In reality this ability to communicate with the local people through a common language rather than through an interpreter, which was also a requirement in many other countries of the empire, was a crucial ingredient in winning their trust and confidence.

By this time not only was I married but we also had our first child, Fiona. This caused a bit of a problem because there was no provision in the regulations for a District Officer Cadet on first appointment to be accompanied by a wife, let alone a child. So a special dispensation had to be obtained in writing from the Secretary of State for the Colonies.

Having obtained the Secretary of State's approval, we joined the Union Castle liner *Kenya Castle* in August 1958 in Genoa. There were some ten other cadets en route to their first postings in Tanganyika. We were under no illusion that the Empire would last for ever – Ghana had already become independent a year before we sailed. As long ago as 1925 the then Governor of Tanganyika, Sir Donald Cameron, said 'We are here on behalf of the League of Nations to teach Africans to stand by themselves. When they can do that, we must get out. It will take a long time, yet everything we do must be based on this principle.' Indeed it was never in doubt that our underlying purpose was to bring Tanganyika to independence as soon as it was ready. The key question was however one of timing. Like many of my contemporaries I thought that, as Tanganyika was much less developed than the West African colonies and indeed than Kenya and Uganda, there would probably be a useful job to do for at least ten years. Certainly none of us were prepared for the speed of change in Tanganyika after 1958, and during a week of briefings in Dar es Salaam we were given little inkling of it.

Initially Val and I were allocated separate cabins. However two of the other cadets, none of whom were married at that time, swapped with us so that Val and I and Fiona could all be together. There was no air conditioning in the cabin and it was like an oven when we reached the Red Sea. Consequently we had to spend much of our time on deck. Our main concern was keeping Fiona from falling overboard. Then aged just sixteen months she could toddle everywhere and was into everything.

I had three postings during our three year tour, all of them in the then Central Province. The first was to Kondoa Irangi, an old Arab trading post on the slave route from Zanzibar to the interior. It had grown up round a freshwater spring on the bank of a sand river and was dominated by a splendid Beau Geste style fort built by the Germans. Under the British it now served as the District Office or boma.

The main tribe in the district were the Warangi, a Bantu people who were both pastoralists and maize farmers. They had a destructively large population of goats which, over the years, had contributed to serious soil erosion. This was most apparent in the multitude of 'korongos', steep sided ravines caused by rainy season streams washing away the bare soil. We tried hard, without much success, to persuade the Warangi to reduce their herds of goats.

In the town of Kondoa itself most of the people were Muslim. But further out in the district they still held to their traditional tribal beliefs. However, there was a strong Catholic missionary presence in the south and in the remote Sandawe country (see below). The missionaries were mainly Passionist Fathers from Bergamo in Italy and I had much admiration for them. They built churches from scratch. I remember one particularly fine one in Lalta in Sandawe country. They also tried to provide some basic education and health care for the local people where there was little or none. Nor, unlike some other missionary organizations, did they ask for help from the government. At the same time they managed to produce wine and make their own salami!

We lived in a simple mud-brick bungalow with a tin roof under-slung by lengths of hessian painted white to keep out the heat. There was no electricity but we had the luxury of (cold) running water from a storage tank further up the hill. We also had the luxury of a fridge which ran quite efficiently on paraffin. For light at night we had Petromax pressure lamps. Hot water came from a 'Tanganyika boiler', an old 44-gallon oil drum filled with water which was attached to the outside wall of the house and heated underneath by firewood. A pipe carried the water straight through the wall and into the bath. The kitchen was in a thatched hut about twenty yards behind the house which contained a wood-burning 'Dover' stove.

Val made sure that we grew our own vegetables. We bought eggs, milk and an occasional scrawny chicken from the local Warangi farmers. The nearest grocery store, Fatehali Dhala, was a hundred miles away in Dodoma over a heavily corrugated dirt road. We were lucky as grapes and other fresh fruit were provided by a remarkable survivor from the first world war, Herr Tschoepe (we never knew his first name). He had been the driver of the only truck in General von Lettow Vorbeck's army. After the war he had stayed on and settled down in Kondoa where in due course he had become the water engineer (Bwana Maji) for the local district council. Tschoepe spoke an almost unintelligible mix of heavily accented English, broad Silesian-German, which even Val had difficulty in understanding, and kitchen Swahili.

While I could function fairly fluently in Swahili having had the benefit of the language training on the Devonshire course at Oxford, Val struggled a bit at first though she quickly picked it up. On one occasion she caused considerable amusement among a gang of prisoners who were supposed to be planting a particular type of hedge to protect our shamba from cattle and other animals. It so happens that the Swahili words for that particular plant (mnyara) and for village headman (mnyapara) are similar. Inadvertently she ended up telling the gang that it was very important to plant the headmen in straight lines. It made their day.

Worse was to follow as a result of a misunderstanding between Val and our willing, but inexperienced, Irangi cook, Ali. The occasion was our very first dinner party at which the principal guest was the visiting Provincial Commissioner, next only to the Governor in the hierarchy. All went well until the fish course which did not arrive. Never mind, we just carried on with the main course which was perfectly acceptable. Then came the dessert which Val had explained to Ali in much detail – Queen of Pudding. It looked magnificent but as she dug down through layers of cream, custard and jam there emerged to view a large steamed fish, head and all. Fortunately the assembled guests including the PC saw the funny side.

There was no such thing as television or telephones and even local radio reception was faint and intermittent. Our only means of communication with the outside world was via a radio signal which was open for half-an-hour a day. For entertainment we had a Deccalian gramophone run off a car battery. We also acquired in due course a young orphan Rhesus monkey, a large chameleon and a very stupid but good natured Rhodesian Ridgeback called Fausto. The monkey teased Fausto constantly – his favourite trick being to jump off the table on to Fausto's back as he walked past and pull his ears and then jump back again before Fausto had time to work out what was happening. But the chameleon was more than a match for the monkey which it terrified by turning jet black whenever the monkey came anywhere near it. Eventually the monkey had to go (to a game scout) because it became jealous of Fiona and on one occasion actually attacked her by coming up behind her and scratching her face with its front paws.

Apart from our Irangi cook, we also had an ayah to help Val to look after Fiona. She came from the click-speaking Wasandawe people who until very recently had been hunter gatherers. They lived in the most remote and least developed part of the District. Yet she was a wonderfully attentive ayah. At the time, and until she eventually forgot how to make the clicks, Fiona must have been the only European child anywhere except perhaps southern African who could understand and say a few words in a click language.

Although Kondoa itself was virtually an oasis in a rocky, semi desert area, it was also on the edge of the great Serengeti plains. From the top of the Kolo escarpment just to the north of us we could gaze across it to the snow-capped cone of Kilimanjaro 170 miles away. To this day that view remains the grandest I have ever seen. On either side of the main road north to Arusha there was a profusion of antelope, ostrich, wildebeest and giraffe with the occasional herd of elephants for good measure. The whole effect was like a giant open air zoo. It never occurred to us that within a generation it would have vanished.

Apart from Herr Tschoepe there were about half-a-dozen other Europeans on the station including my boss Richard Brayne, his wife Anne and their two young children. All of us were government employees and part of the district team charged with the administration and development of the District in conjunction with the local district Council and the village headmen.

As a newly arrived District Officer Cadet I was given special responsibility for the Wasandawe people. The area was separated from the rest of the district, where the majority Warangi lived, by a belt of tsetse infested bush. Consequently anyone entering or leaving it by the one barely motorable track had to drive with the windows tightly shut, not a pleasant experience in the days before vehicles had air conditioning. They also had to pass through a fly disinfestation chamber at either end. Inside the chamber the vehicle was sprayed with copious quantities of DDT. At that time there was little awareness of the health risks to the occupants let alone the tsetse control staff themselves.

Because of its isolation the Sandawe country was virtually untouched by the outside world. On one occasion when I had managed to reach far into the bush beyond Kwa Mtoro with the Land Rover it soon became apparent that some of the local people had never seen a vehicle of any kind close up. After curiosity overcame their initial suspicion I was cross questioned about it. 'Whose donkey (punda) is it? What does it eat?'

One of my first tasks was to review several coroners' inquests which had been left unresolved. The victims all had in common that they had been found lying dead in the bush with claw marks on their bodies indicating that they had been attacked by a lion. There were known to be one or more man-eating lions in Sandawe country but there was also a lion-man cult in the area. This was a truly evil practice which enabled a witch doctor to 'acquire' a young male child and train him to develop into a so-called lion man by keeping him in a remote cave, clothing him only in lion skin and feeding him on raw meat. Once fully grown the witch doctor could then hire out his 'lion-man' to carry out contract killings on behalf of individuals who wished to take revenge for some real or imagined harm they had suffered. The murder would then be passed off as the act of a man-eating lion.

The difficulty with the inquests was that there were rarely any reliable witnesses or indeed any witnesses at all. Furthermore it was virtually impossible to distinguish between claw marks made by a lion, which could be remarkably precise, and those made by a 'lion man' using the claws of his lion skin. Also it was well established that a lion would sometimes kill its victim with one blow and then drag the body into the bush before returning later to eat it. Consequently it was not possible to find enough evidence to justify calling for an individual to be charged with murder or even with aiding and abetting a murder.

The system provided for the tribal headmen and elders to be responsible for dealing with minor crime and transgressions in accordance with customary law, but serious crime including murder or manslaughter was reserved for trial under English law. Under this system district officers were appointed as magistrates class 1, 2 or 3 according to their seniority and proficiency in the law, and the penalties they could impose were graded accordingly. For example a magistrate grade 3, which I was for most of my tour, could only impose a maximum prison sentence of six months. The most serious cases, eg murder, were reserved for hearing by professional resident magistrates who toured the districts from the provincial capital. But it fell to the district officers to conduct preliminary inquiries to decide whether a case should be referred upwards for trial by the resident magistrate. There was also a right of appeal from the courts to the High Court in Dar es Salaam. Incidentally, apart from issues reserved to be dealt with by Africans under customary law, the law of the land, based on English common law and the Indian Penal Code, applied equally to all races including Europeans.

One day in our next district Val was threatened in our kitchen by an African holding a knife to her chest. He was an acquaintance of our cook and had called in for a chat. But he lost his temper over something my wife had said to him about letting the cook get on with his cooking. In the event Val walked towards him to get out of the room and he was so surprised that he backed away. When Val told me what had happened I felt that it was my duty to report the incident. Consequently the perpetrator was charged under a provision of the Indian Penal code (which was applied in Tanganyika) that it was a criminal offence to behave in such a way as to cause a reasonable person to be in fear of their life. The case was then referred to a European magistrate whose first question to my wife was 'were you afraid?'. At the time she had not been afraid (though her knees were shaking afterwards) and she honestly answered 'no'. Whereupon the magistrate immediately dismissed the case and the accused walked free. Critics of the evils of the British Empire as it was in those days might reflect on whether such an outcome could possibly have happened under an oppressive regime.

After a year in Kondoa I was transferred to Mpwapwa district, some sixty miles to the east of Dodoma, where the Wagogo, a cattle-owning people like the Masai, were the dominant tribe. Mpwapwa itself was a thriving trading centre. It was also the location of the veterinary research centre for the Territory which had originally been established by the Germans before the First World War when Tanganyika was a German *schutzgebiet*. Mpwapwa also boasted an important teacher training college. Consequently there were many more Europeans than in Kondoa-enough to sustain a club with a tennis court and a small swimming pool. We also had the luxury of a generator which provided electricity for about four hours in the evening, and a nine-hole golf course albeit with browns rather than greens. We were housed in a proper stone bungalow dating from the days of the German protectorate..

It was deliciously cool after the rigours of our mud brick abode in Kondoa. We were even more fortunate in finding a wonderful cook/houseboy, Paolo, with whom we stayed in touch until he died many years later.

My DC, Michael Sword, insisted that we should each aim to spend at least ten days a month on safari in order to keep closely in touch with the people throughout the district. In my case this included going on foot safari into the mountainous area in the south of the district where there were no roads and some of the paths were precipitous. It was hot and tiring work but it brought me into contact with the proud Wahehe warrior tribe who only some fifty years earlier had wiped out a column of German Schutztruppe. On such occasions I would take with me only my cook and a messenger from the district office together with a tent and a few cooking utensils.

During the day I would check the tax books and perhaps count the cash in the local baraza and then listen to people's 'shidas'(problems) and explain what the government was doing, or trying to do, about providing for example another dispensary for the area, or a primary school. In the evening we might sit around a camp fire chatting with some of the local headmen and anyone else who chose to turn up. This was a relationship totally unknown to today's international experts with the exception of a few dedicated volunteers with some of the NGOs.

Although Val did not accompany me on these safaris she was kept pretty busy, not least in translating some of the German veterinary archives which we managed to obtain from Berlin. From these it soon became apparent that at least some of the research which had been, and was still being done, by the British at Mpwapwa had already been carried out by the Germans. In other words we were putting a good deal of time and effort into reinventing the wheel. Among many discoveries in these archives was a section on attempts to tame zebras complete with a remarkable photograph of a German officer riding one. I assume this endeavour was motivated by the fact that large areas of Tanganyika were off limits to horses because of the prevalence of tsetse fly to which horses were susceptible.

I suppose many of us have experienced what a small world it is when we unexpectedly bump into someone we know in a faraway place. Most memorably it happened to me on safari in Mpwapwa District. I was walking along a dried-up river bed looking for a possible site for a small dam which could retain water from the rainy season through the dry season. On rounding a bend in the river bed I came face to face with an old school chum walking in the opposite direction. In such a remote place it was almost like a Stanley and Livingstone moment. It turned out that he, rather more ambitiously, was looking for diamonds. In the event neither of us found what we were looking for.

Just to the north of Mpwapwa was the sub-district of Kongwa, scene of the ill-fated groundnut scheme in 1950. After a year in Mpwapwa I was appointed district officer in charge at Kongwa, a semi-independent command. All that remained of the groundnut scheme was the Tanganyika Agricultural Corporation ranch on some 15,000 acres of land which had been cleared for the scheme, together with a well-equipped government hospital and a few tarmac roads leading nowhere.

The groundnut scheme itself was an ambitious post-war project which failed mainly because of the arrogance of the Whitehall scientists and mandarins who drove it. Rationing was still in force in the UK and butter was scarce. So the scheme was partly intended to provide the British housewife with ready access to margarine which could be cheaply made with groundnuts as a main ingredient. It was also intended to pave the way for African farmers in the area to farm on a commercial scale. The plan was to clear about 150,000 acres of bush in Kongwa and plant groundnuts on an industrial scale using fleets of bulldozers and tractors. In the event only about 15,000 acres were ever cleared, the groundnuts failed to germinate because the rainfall was too low and the rainy season too short, and the imported machinery could not cope with the African bush. The local inhabitants and indeed the administration could have warned Whitehall of this outcome if they had been properly consulted which, according to the many veterans of the scheme to whom I spoke, they were not.

It is however worth pointing out that the scheme was paid for by the British taxpayer at a cost of over 30 million pounds(about a billion pounds in today's money), and that it led to the establishment of the Tanganyika Agricultural Corporation ranch on the land which had been cleared.

We had one of the few modern bungalows still standing. It was pretty isolated and I vividly recall the chilling laugh of hyenas circling it at night. Large black scorpions, the size of small crayfish, were another speciality of the place. They clattered across the stone floor of the bungalow and were too big to be squashed underfoot. However I found that the heavy wooden government-issue waste paper box was ideal for dropping on to them. They could at least be easily heard and seen and were reputedly less venomous than the smaller variety. They could move very fast. On one occasion a scorpion climbed on to Val's unshod foot. It took great presence of mind on her part to remain motionless until it climbed off again and I was able to dispose of it.

Our son, Robert, was born in June 1961 towards the end of our tour. Val went to the mission hospital at Mvumi, near Dodoma, for the delivery. At that time the maternity unit was run by a well-known obstetrician, Dr Taylor, who had given up his Harley Street practice to serve in Tanganyika. Robert was one of the very few European babies ever to have been born there.

Two months later, in August 1961, we left Tanganyika for good shortly after I had handed over in Kongwa to one of the first African district officers. Val and I had both had the experience of a lifetime and had grown fond of the country and of its people. But with independence due in December I had decided that, notwithstanding the then Prime Minister Julius Nyerere's persuasive personal letter inviting me and my administrative officer colleagues to stay on,* the needs of the family had to come first. This may sound selfish, and maybe it was, but I also thought that for the transition phase it was the more experienced white administrative officers who would be most needed while the more junior posts could, and should, be filled by local African trainees.

During our three years in Tanganyika the pace of political change had accelerated dramatically. By 1960 the Territory already had self-government and it was announced that it would be granted full independence (*uhuru*) in December 1961. It had of course long been recognised that independence was coming but we in the administration had serious misgivings about the time-scale for it. However pressure was building both from within, as TANU led by Julius Nyerere was becoming more assertive and self-confident, and internationally from the United States and from the UN Trusteeship Committee. The latter had the right to review progress to independence because of Tanganyika's status as a UN Trust Territory. The whole process was also speeded up by the enthusiasm of the remarkable Secretary of State for the Colonies, Iain Macleod, who was keen to bring the colonies to independence as quickly as possible. As the date for

---

* See Appendix A.

independence drew nearer the atmosphere was good humoured and full of hope for the future. The usual Swahili greeting of 'jambo' was replaced by 'uhuru' meaning freedom. My elderly father in law, on a visit, caused only roars of good humoured laughter when he would reply, wagging his finger, 'na kazi' meaning 'and work', the other half of the TANU slogan which most of the people conveniently chose to forget.

In the same year that Tanganyika experienced a peaceful transition to self-government, the Belgian Congo exploded into violence and Belgium withdrew in a panic leaving chaos behind. The event sent shock waves through the white and Asian communities in Tanganyika though most people believed, rightly, that the contagion would not spread. Most ordinary Tanganyika Africans were revolted at the brutality shown by some of the Congolese people towards the white population. A special train was laid on from Kigoma to Dar es Salaam to carry Belgian refugees, who had fled across Lake Tanganyika to escape the killing. In striking contrast to the scenes in the Congo, it was besieged along the way by groups of local Africans offering gifts of fruit and other food to the passengers. We know because along with other volunteers we met the train when it arrived at Dar where we happened to be spending a week's local leave.

In an ideal world independence should have been delayed by at least another ten years. There were far too few qualified doctors, teachers, engineers or other professionals and virtually no middle class. Education, even to primary school level, was still far from universal and secondary schools were few and far between. There was no university though Makerere in Kampala, which was regarded as one of the best universities in Africa, served Tanganyika as well as Kenya and Uganda. Perhaps most critically there were far too few African administrators and no African magistrates or judges. In July 1961 only just over 12% of responsible positions in the public service were occupied by Africans, and there were far too few in the other professions.

Against such a lack of preparation it looks almost foolhardy for the Governor, Sir Richard Turnbull, to have recommended giving Tanganyika its independence as early as December 1961 and for the British government to have agreed. On the other hand there was an expectation that a fair number of experienced British administrators and other professionals would stay on (see Nyerere's invitation above) and provide a temporary framework of government until Africans were ready to take their place. In the event some did so but not for very long as the pressure from TANU for Africanisation of the Civil Service became too great.

It is also clear that there could be no such thing as the right moment to hand over. The momentum for change in Africa was growing well before Harold Macmillan's 'winds of change' speech in 1960. It should have been apparent after Ghana was granted independence in 1957 that Britain's other African territories, however varied their state of development, could not be far behind. As explained above, pressure from the US, Britain's closest ally, to get out grew stronger after the Suez debacle, and also from the UN. Although we were hardly conscious of it in up-country Mpwapwa, there was also growing impatience within Tanganyika particularly in the towns. Although initially willing to wait for several years, Nyerere was quick to see the way the wind was blowing and to recognise that he had to be seen to take the lead.

In my view the following quotation from a conversation between the then Prime Minister, Harold Macmillan, on a visit to Ghana and Nigeria in 1960, and an unnamed colonial administrator with many years experience in the Colonial Service illustrates why it would have been wrong to delay. When Macmillan asked him whether he thought that the local people were ready for independence he replied ' no, of course they are not ready for it. They are learning fast but it will take at least fifteen or twenty years before their leaders are ready to take full responsibility'. When asked what then he would advise he replied without hesitation 'I would give it to them at once – as soon as possible'. When Macmillan expressed surprise at this response he explained 'If the fifteen or twenty years were to be applied in learning the job, in increasing their experience of local government or of central administration why then I would be all for it. But that is not what will happen. All the most intelligent men capable of government will be in rebellion. I will have to put them in prison. There they will learn nothing about administration, only about hatred and revenge. They will not be fruitful, but wasted years; so I say give independence now.'*

One other reflection stands out. My experience of British rule in Tanganyika at grass roots level was that the main purpose of our being there was to encourage and promote development in all its forms. Indeed, apart

---

* From Harold Macmillan's autobiography: "Pointing the Way".

from a wish to avoid the tedium of a nine-to-five office job in the UK, and a wish for a bit of adventure, my main motivation, and I believe that of most of my colleagues, was to help to speed up the economic development of the local people and improve their lives. Of course law and order needed to be maintained and taxes had to be collected so that government could function. But a major part of our daily routine consisted of working with the local council and village headmen to establish and maintain local dispensaries, district roads, markets, earth dams and local schools. In most districts, apart from the administration, there was usually an agricultural officer charged, for example, with improving animal husbandry, siting boreholes, and encouraging crop rotation and terracing. Other staff included a district medical officer and perhaps a water or PWD engineer and a veterinary officer. Education, though still inadequate, was also a priority.

Apart from the work being done at grass-roots level it is often forgotten that at the height of the Second World War, when we were fighting for our very survival, the British government passed a Colonial Development and Welfare Act in 1940 and another one in 1945. Although the amounts were modest these released funds paid for by the British taxpayer for development in the colonies. The focus was on expanding agricultural production and research and also helping to stimulate investment. In Jamaica for example they financed the founding of part of the University of the West Indies. They also provided investment in a sugar refinery and a cement factory. More significantly they demonstrated that the government recognised that it had a joint responsibility with the colonies themselves to contribute to their economic development.

Yet there has grown up a widely believed myth that somehow 'development', a word which has acquired a mystique all its own, only began after independence. It is entirely understandable that this myth should have been fostered by the respective governments of the newly-independent countries. It is however not so apparent why Britain should have bought into it unless from a misplaced sense of guilt and a wish to please the governments of the former colonies.

As I have said there is also a widespread misconception in this country that colonial rule was universally harsh and oppressive, and that the colonies only won their independence through a freedom struggle. It may indeed have been quite harsh in the early days, especially where white settlers were encouraged to take possession of the best land and start farming as in Kenya, though nothing like as severe as in the German territories. But in most British territories in Africa government was carried out with a far lighter touch than they have experienced after independence. Indirect rule has been widely criticised as a cynical device for saving money and indeed for suppressing the indigenous people. But the critics cannot have it both ways. By definition it did not provide a mechanism for running an oppressive and highly centralised regime since it depended heavily on local chiefs and local native authorities. In reality government was only possible because of the willing cooperation of the vast majority of the people. The notion that Tanganyika, for example, could have been held down by force against the will of the people is absurd. All that the government had at its disposal was a tiny police force, almost entirely Tanganyikan, with one battalion of the Kings African Rifles, also composed of local African askaris with some British officers. This for a territory nearly twice the size of France.

As for the various so-called freedom struggles, they were almost entirely political and peaceful rather than violent. It is worth recalling that there were hundreds of thousands of Africans and West Indians under arms at the end of the war who had volunteered to fight for the Empire. It evidently never occurred to them that they had a splendid opportunity to seize their freedom by force of arms if they had chosen to do so.

Some statistics quoted by the late Anthony Kirk-Greene in his book *On Crown Service* show that in the late thirties Tanganyika had only 185 expatriate Administrative officers for the whole territory. Even more remarkably there were only 120 expatriate police and military personnel. Although the numbers no doubt increased somewhat after the war they would never have been enough to enforce an oppressive regime. The figures Kirk-Greene quotes for all of Britain's African colonies and protectorates are even more remarkable – 1123 and 938 expatriates respectively. To put them into some kind of perspective Kent County Council currently employs some 6,000 full time staff not including the police force! [*figures from KCC Workforce Profile*]

The nature of the relationship between the supposedly oppressive colonial regime and the incoming independent government in Tanganyika is perhaps best epitomised in the personal letter from the then Prime Minister (shortly to be President of the new Republic), Julius Nyerere, to which I have earlier referred. In his eloquent appeal to each administrative officer to stay on he says 'We need our experienced administrators, our corps d'elite as the

Governor called you the other day, because it is they who keep the whole machinery of Government working.' In his long letter he also appeals to 'the sense of mission which our Administrative Officers have always felt'. He also thanks those who are leaving 'for what you have done'. This is not the kind of letter which could possibly have been written from the incoming leader of an independent country which had suffered from years of colonial oppression. The reality is that the relationship between British and Tanganyikans on the ground, at least in the last days of British rule, was based on mutual respect. We respected them and I believe that on the whole they respected us.

The cement in the relationship between government and governed was provided by the district officers and their teams of specialists living among the local people and for the most part speaking a common language. In East Africa that was usually Swahili or, in some places, the local tribal language. Contrast that with the situation today with large numbers of development specialists flitting in and out of a country for a few days and mainly staying in the best hotels in the cities. Not only do they have little understanding of the local people but equally the inhabitants have little or no understanding of, or trust in, them. Not surprising then that so often their recipes for 'development' do not work. The late Ross Coggins' highly critical poem 'The Development Set', though written many years ago, sums it up perfectly. [reproduced in Graham Hancock's 'Lords of Poverty', see annex B].

In practice government had to be, and was, by consent even if it was not democratic. I well remember how on one occasion in Kondoa I was required to go out and arrest five Masai warriors who were suspected of cattle rustling. This was quite a common phenomenon on the edges of Masai country because the Masai had the convenient belief that God had given all the cattle in the world to them. I had with me in the office Land Rover Val, our little blonde daughter Fiona, and a messenger from the boma. We came upon the Masai resting on their spears at a remote borehole where they had taken the cattle to drink. As soon as we got out of the car they formed a circle round our little girl and started spitting on her head. We could see from their body language that they were not hostile, and later we discovered that they had never seen a European child before and that the spitting was a sign of blessing. In any case I then had to tell the messenger to inform them that they were under arrest and should get into the back of the Land Rover pick-up truck to be taken to the local prison in Kondoa (generally known in local parlance as Her Majesty's hoteli) to await trial for cattle rustling.

Fortunately they seemed happy to comply, partly perhaps because they were excited at the prospect of a ride in a vehicle. It certainly never occurred to me nor, more importantly, to them that they could just have told me to get lost. Had they chosen to do so there was no plan B.

Nor was government in Tanganyika racist, in the sense of believing in some kind of innate superiority of the white man, though undeniably there were individual officers who thought that way. It was, however, paternalistic, which is not at all the same thing, but was based on the view that Africans needed to be protected from some aspects of the modern world until such time as they were able, through education and contact, to deal with it on equal terms. Thus there was, for example, a Native Protection Ordinance which was designed to protect Africans from the activities of unscrupulous Indian and European traders and money lenders.

It is interesting to compare this attitude to that of President Museveni of Uganda many years later, whom I often heard refer to 'my backward people'. In so doing he did not mean to imply that they are in any way inferior to anyone else, but simply that many Ugandans still lacked some of the education and skills which we in the West take for granted.

I am not trying to justify colonialism but I do believe that British colonialism, with all its shortcomings, was more benign than most, and that as practised in most of the colonies in the last few decades of Empire it was well intentioned, responsible and on the whole beneficial. Most importantly, especially when one compares it with the situation in many African countries today, it was not corrupt. Furthermore one has to ask what realistic alternative would there have been at the time?

Clearly in some cases, not least in Tanganyika, we left before the country was adequately prepared for independence. But in exiting from empire as we did, we not only opened the way for the former colonies to become full members of the Commonwealth, but also ensured that in most cases the achievement of independence was peaceful. This is in contrast with the experience of other colonial powers, notably France and Portugal.

The contemporary cultural criticism in Britain about our colonial past does us no favours nor indeed the generations of inhabitants of the former Empire around the world without whose cooperation and support the Empire could never have been sustained. Years later in Uganda I was told on a number of occasions by older Ugandans how they looked back to the years of British rule as a golden age of peace and progress. Cynics will argue that they would of course say that out of politeness or a wish to please, which are characteristics of Ugandan culture and perhaps African culture more widely. I happen to believe however that the sentiment was genuine.

But do not take my word for it. Here is what Chinua Achebe, the great Nigerian novelist and critic of Empire had to say. 'Here is a heresy: The British governed their colony of Nigeria with considerable care' and he goes on 'It is important to face the fact that the British colonies, more or less, were expertly run.' Yet more significantly, and doubtless to the surprise of many ill informed critics of the colonial empire, he argues in his last book '*There was a country: A personal history of Biafra*' that a key reason for the weakness of the state in Nigeria is that it repudiated too much of the colonial legacy inherited from the British.

Even more strikingly the former Prime Minister of India, Dr Manmohan Singh, speaking in Oxford in 2005 spoke positively about India's experience with Britain during the days of the Raj. 'Our notions of the rule of law, of a Constitutional government, of a free press, of a professional civil service, of modern universities and research laboratories ... are all elements that we still value and cherish. Our judiciary, our legal system, our bureaucracy and our police are all great institutions derived from British-Indian administration and they have served our country exceedingly well.'

Chapter 5

The ICI Years

On returning to the UK we were fortunate to be able to stay in a little cottage near Colchester which was an annex to a lovely house and garden owned by my Uncle Harry (the same one who had been my guardian) and Aunt Hilda. From there I had to start job hunting in earnest. For Val and me settling back to living in the UK was not too much of an ordeal having only been away for three years. For Fiona, now aged four and a half, it was all entirely new and it took a while for her to realise that life was going to be very different from the more laid back style she had known in Tanganyika. On a visit with her to London a few weeks after we had arrived home we went shopping in Oxford Street. In one of the department stores she suddenly disappeared. After a worrying few moments we heard her exclaim loudly from inside a shop window where she had gone to have a good look at the mannequins, 'Mummy, this Mummy's got no panties on.' The many shoppers around must have wondered what sort of parents this child had.

About two months after leaving Tanganyika, in October 1961, I accepted an offer from the Nobel Division of ICI to join the Personnel Department at the company's huge explosives complex at Ardeer on the Ayrshire coast. The complex, which covered several hundred acres of sand dunes, had originally been established before the First World War. It quickly grew to be at one time one of the largest explosives factories in the world.

Moving from Africa to Scotland at the onset of winter and plunging into the harsh reality of the trade union world was a bit of a culture shock. While looking for a house to buy Val and I rented part of a seaside bungalow in the suburb of Barassie just outside Troon. Our landlady was a formidable personage with a heart of gold, Miss McLean. On our first day she asked me, somewhat to my surprise, 'When do you like to take a bath?' When I answered, fresh as I was from the tropical heat of Tanganyika, that I usually took a bath in the morning it was her turn to look surprised. 'I mean which day' she explained in her broad Scots. I had not realised that she had to light the coal-fired boiler specially to heat the water for a bath. Another surprise awaited us in the sitting room where we found that we had to weigh the corners of the carpet down with bricks to stop it from billowing upwards as it was lifted by the westerly gales whistling through the cracks between the floor boards and the ventilators below them.

After several months with Miss McClean we bought a sturdy semi-detached house in Prestwick overlooking the golf course and the sea. There, as in Barassie, we made some good friends, both neighbours and fellow employees of ICI. It may have helped that neither of us were Sassenachs. One lesson I learned was that the Scots were not only very careful with their own money but also with other people's money. On one occasion Val wanted to send a particular magazine by express post to her mother who was in hospital in Germany. But the lady in the local post office told her firmly 'och no ye cannie dae that'. 'Why not?' said Val thinking there might be some regulation about sending papers by express post. 'Its far too expensive', came the reply. A few years later when we moved to join ICI Europa in London I asked the manager of the NatWest branch, where I was opening an account, if I could have the same overdraft arrangement as I had previously had with the local branch of the Bank of Scotland in Prestwick. 'Of course you can', he said. 'Whatever arrangement you have with the Bank of Scotland I am sure we can do at least the same for you here.' He never asked what the arrangement was. How things have changed!

Nobel Division itself was still in the throes of down-sizing after the Second World War and had not managed to find a major new product capable of taking up the slack, though production of silicone had looked promising for a time. Consequently there was an on-going programme of redundancies, euphemistically called premature retirement or what the workers referred to as people being 'retired prematurely early before their time'. There were constant demarcation disputes between the craft unions in particular who were anxious to protect their share of a dwindling amount of work. In the main production plants, working with nitroglycerine, black powder and detonators to make commercial explosives, the work was hard and occasionally lethal. Despite stringent precautions, explosions in the scattered huts of the Blasting Department, carefully sited well away among the sand dunes, were not unknown and usually resulted in at least two or three deaths. They were pretty gruesome events as the victims were literally blown to pieces. With hindsight it is quite remarkable that anyone was willing to do such work for a fairly modest wage. Virtually all the detonator production was done by young women because their fingers were more nimble so they could work more quickly and efficiently than the men.

Interestingly it was the custom among the men working in the Blasting Department to smear the inside of their flat caps with a little nitroglycerine whenever they had a few days off work for holidays or sickness. Medical science of course now knows that nitroglycerine helps to thin the blood and therefore provides a measure of protection against strokes and heart attacks. But the men did not know this at the time. Nevertheless it is reasonable to assume that a few men at least who were suffering from undiagnosed heart or circulation problems which were disguised by their exposure to nitroglycerine, were in fact kept alive by this simple habit.

Against this background it is hardly surprising that morale was low. The situation was not helped by the management's attempts to apply the mechanistic discipline of 'work study' linked to bonus schemes in an effort to improve productivity. As the systems were imposed from above there was little sense of ownership of them on the shop floor. As one feisty shop steward put it, 'Yez will have tae bring in the military if yez want tae get that in here.'

Away from the factory we greatly enjoyed exploring Scotland, especially the Highlands, even though at the time money was very tight. The food may have been a bit ordinary in those days but we both fell in love with Scottish music and dancing and the special magic of Hogmanay. We have been back many times.

After three years in Ardeer I transferred to the recently established ICI Europa in London whose role was to oversee and coordinate the proliferating subsidiary companies on the continent. Shortly afterwards it was decided that it would be more appropriate to locate ICI Europa's Headquarters in Brussels. Accordingly I found myself, with one of the company's legal advisers, given the task of finding a suitable office in Brussels and recruiting local staff to provide back up for the senior staff moving across from London. In my desire to ensure the best quality of local staff I set their starting salaries rather higher than they should have been! The local staff were quite happy though the management of ICI Europa were not so pleased. But we had been given a free rein and virtually no guidance from Head Office in Millbank as to what was expected.

One never to be forgotten memory from those days is of our son, Robert, then aged six, slipping inside a hollow letter box at our front gate in the posh suburb of Uccle and squirting water from a syringe through the slit at local people waiting at a nearby bus stop. The resulting spectacle of portly Belgians side-stepping on the pavement was hilarious. Fortunately a bus came along before they discovered where the water came from but of course, despite the temptation, we had to make sure that he did not repeat the performance. Robert never took kindly to learning French which he seemed to think had been specially invented to make life difficult for him. After one term at a local French-speaking school his class mistress told us in her report that unfortunately he had not learned very much French but they had all learned a lot of English!

After barely six months in Brussels I was asked to take over the job of Group Personnel Manager for the ICI group of companies in Malaysia and Singapore based in Kuala Lumpur. I jumped at the chance of seeing a new part of the world and returning to warmer climes. So once more we found ourselves sailing from Genoa, this time on board the Hapag Lloyd's 'Combi' ship the MV *Hamburg*. This turned out to be far more comfortable than the old *Kenya Castle* which did not even have air conditioned cabins. The *Hamburg* only took forty passengers so we all got to know each other rather well. The ship's leisurely voyage was made even slower as we were becalmed in the Indian Ocean for several days while the ship 'drew a piston'. Among our fellow passengers was Baron von Richthofen, nephew of the famous fighter ace of the First World War, who was en route to take up his post as the FRG Ambassador in Singapore. He and his family proved to be delightful travelling companions.

We eventually disembarked at Port Swettenham as it then was (now Port Klang), not without incident. The first shock was to discover that I should not have included my old shotgun in our baggage as the penalty for possession of a firearm without a licence was death. At the time a state of emergency was still in force because of Malaysia's on-going confrontation with Indonesia. In the event the difficulty was resolved by handing the offending weapon over to the police for safe-keeping. We had another shock three days later when we discovered that the ship had sailed on to Singapore without off-loading our precious possessions, and furthermore that she was going on from there to be broken up for scrap at Pusan in South Korea! Apparently it had rained incessantly at Port Swettenham and the captain had decided that he could not afford to damage the cargo in the hold by opening the hatches (this was of course long before the advent of containers). At all events there followed a flurry of telephone calls to the manager of ICI Singapore who somehow managed to arrange for our possessions to be off loaded in the harbour and transferred to another vessel bound for Europe via Port Swettenham. We were much relieved to be able to pick them up from there several days later.

After a couple of moves we settled in to a modest house in a terrace of four with a view over some disused tin mines at Jalan Ampang. The location had the advantage as we saw it of being on the outskirts of town near the jungle at Gombak and mercifully away from the posh and hierarchical suburb of Kenny Hill, home to company chairmen or 'number ones' as they were called in the stratified social world of Kuala Lumpur in the late sixties. We were also fortunate in finding a marvellously capable and efficient Chinese amah, Ah Kieng, who stayed with us throughout our time in Malaysia.

The city itself was still relatively small and green but thriving, with a vibrant business centre where the numerous, mainly British, expatriates were dominant while the Chinese ran the informal sector. Rubber and oil palm were king and European trading and plantation companies such as Barlow Boustead, Harrison and Crossfield, Guthries, Sime Darby and Socfin were household names. Although there was a policy of Malaysianisation, and work permits for expatriates were becoming increasingly hard to obtain, the chairmen and managing directors of the leading companies were almost entirely expatriate. The ICI group had six directors of whom five were British with one token Malay. Most of the plantations were still run by British planters of the old school.

Social life in KL revolved around three clubs from the colonial era. The oldest and most prestigious was the Selangor Club with its cricket pitch right in the centre of town. It was affectionately known as 'the dog'. Then there was the Royal Selangor Club and, for families, the Lake Club. There were no supermarkets in those days but not far from us there was a Chinese general grocery store, Hok Choon. It was there that my innocent idea of the Chinese as imbued with an ancient culture of politeness was rudely shattered. On entering the store for the first time a young female shop assistant shouted loudly from behind the counter 'what you wan?' When I failed to respond immediately with a ready list of items she just moved on to the next customer.

However, we quickly adapted to life in Malaysia and made many friends. The children were soon happily involved in school life at the Alice Smith School where Val found herself teaching French. More unusually she was at the same time also teaching French at the Alliance Française and German at the Goethe Institut.

Much of my time in ICI was spent negotiating with the trade unions representing a work force which was mainly Indian, overseeing a staff development programme for the group's mainly Chinese executives, and recruiting new staff. Although the group's head office was in KL there was also a large fertiliser plant near the then Port Swettenham which was opened shortly after our arrival by the Prime Minister, the charmingly urbane and anglophile Tunku Abdul Rahman. There were also paint factories at Petaling Njaya near KL and in Singapore, and sales offices in a number of locations throughout the country.

With the internal emergency long over we were able to take full advantage of Malaysia's rich landscape and heritage. We took our local leaves in the country and spent many a week end exploring away from KL. I remember in particular beautiful drives up to the hill station at Fraser's Hill where ICI maintained a bungalow. It was actually a rather gracious Edwardian house with large rooms. On one occasion we were entertained by the band of the Royal Marines on R and R leave from an aircraft carrier which had put in to Singapore. They were staying at another 'bungalow' kept by the Royal Navy for ships' crews needing a bit of shore leave. Memorably it had the motto of the wartime air sea rescue service over the door – 'the sea shall not have them'.

There were other safaris to Malacca, with its unique combination of Portuguese, Dutch and British architecture, to Penang and up the east coast to Kuantan and Khota Bahru. We also visited Malaysia's first national park, the Taman Negara which could only be reached by outboard canoe along the Kuala Tahan river. One day while walking in the jungle near the campsite we heard the unmistakable growl of a nearby tiger. Fortunately our canoe was moored only a few yards away. Never before or since did the family move so fast. Nearer KL itself we experienced the extraordinary Hindu festival of Thaipusam and watched in amazement as the devotees, having first worked themselves into a trance, walked barefoot on burning coals or pushed skewers through their tongues and cheeks. On another occasion I had the privilege of competing in a blowpipe competition in the jungle with the headman of an orang asli (aboriginal) group. Although not surprisingly I lost he insisted on making me a gift of the blowpipe and darts which I still have to this day.

In KL itself there was a lively round of parties for both children and adults where expatriates and Malaysians of all races mixed happily and freely. Shortly after we had arrived we received an invitation to a fancy dress ball at the Lake Club to celebrate New Year. While Val dressed colourfully as a beachcomber, I was carried away by an excess of enthusiasm and decided to go as a stone age hunter. I duly appeared painted with leg make-up and clad only in a rudimentary piece of brown cloth and carrying an old lavatory brush as a club. The only problem was that all the other couples were in evening dress and ball gowns. Never have I been so embarrassed. It was then explained to us that it had been a custom in the past to hold an annual fancy dress ball but for many years people had no longer gone in fancy dress. Only they had never changed the name and in the short time we had been in KL nobody had got around to telling us. It was certainly a lesson never to assume that everything is at it seems. At least I did win the prize.

This settled and apparently peaceful way of life changed dramatically on 13 May 1969 in the aftermath of parliamentary elections. The mainly Chinese opposition party staged a march to celebrate better than expected results in the course of which some pieces of pork were allegedly thrown at Malay bystanders. In the feverish post-election climate this crass action sparked a furious response from Malay youths who literally ran amok in the centre of Kuala Lumpur torching Chinese homes and slaughtering their inhabitants with parangs wherever they could find them. My Chinese secretary had a very narrow escape. Luckily she was given shelter by some neighbours.

It all happened very quickly and there were reports afterwards that a Malay fundamentalist organisation had prepared the ground beforehand and had bussed hundreds of Malay youths into the capital. Whatever the truth, the government was caught completely unawares, as were we. Val and our eight 'year' old son were at the Lake Club on the other side of town when the violence broke out. Somehow she managed to find a way home avoiding the normal route through the centre where streets were already blocked and some houses had been set on fire. That night, and for several nights to come, the sky around us was lit up by the flames of burning houses.

After an initial hiatus the government reacted by calling out the army and imposing a strict 24 hour curfew lifted for an hour or two each day to allow people to get in essential food supplies. This was accompanied by equally strict press censorship. However despite these measures and repeated appeals from the Tunku for calm and restraint the killing and burning still continued for several days and spread to other parts of the country.

In this situation it soon became apparent that food was running out in the Malay kampongs surrounding Kuala Lumpur which had become dependent on food brought out to them by traders from the capital. It fell to the Europeans, who were not a target of the Malay gangs, to organise and distribute food to the kampongs as fast as possible to prevent the villagers descending on the city and ransacking the warehouses. There was a call for volunteers and, together with a number of other expatriates, Val and I offered to help. We were collected each morning for several days by a government Minister who took us in his car through the makeshift barricades and checkpoints to the packing and distribution centre. One morning, as we worked away filling bags with flour in the dust and the heat, we were greatly encouraged by a visit from the Tunku who was greeted by shouts of 'come and join the flour people'. The late sixties was of course the epoch of the flower power generation.

It took several weeks to restore law and order fully throughout the country and bring about a semblance of normality. But I believe that the strict censorship imposed from the outset on press, radio and television was a major factor in preventing a bad situation from getting even worse, or developing into a long running conflict. This was in sharp contrast to the situation in Northern Ireland which Val and I visited shortly afterwards on leave. There the intense media spotlight on victims of violence and their families only added fuel to the flames. It must be questionable whether the general public has a right to see and hear from the victims in all its graphic detail the results of ethnic or religious violence if the effect is to exacerbate the very passions and prejudices which are feeding the violence in the first place. Freedom of the press, like all freedoms in a civilised and democratic society, should in my view not be unlimited, especially when the press seems only to be interested in maximising profits and is unable to use its freedom responsibly.

Before the riots I had recruited a young Malaysian Chinese, Lim Say Chong, to take over from me. Little did I imagine at the time that eventually he would go on to lead a management buy-out of the company and be awarded a Dato-ship for his services to business in Malaysia. We have stayed in touch down the years and he still remains as modest and unassuming as when we first met.

At the end of 1969 we bade a fond farewell to Kuala Lumpur and Malaysia where we had lived happily for three years and had made many friends. In the new year I took up a new job in the Central Personnel Department at ICI's imposing headquarters in Millbank.

The culture at Millbank was old-fashioned and hierarchical. The Main Board Directors, all male of course, were secluded in their grand offices on the top floor where they also had their own dining room. Female staff were largely confined to secretarial or routine office jobs. Sober suits and black shoes were de rigueur. When I once appeared wearing brown shoes I was smartly rebuked by my boss's PA with the comment 'I see we have our engineers' shoes on today.'

Recognising that there was a need for change, the company had embarked on an ambitious programme to introduce American-style management techniques, notably 'Management by Objectives' which was all the rage at the time. The programme was supposed to be master-minded by the Central Personnel Department. However it became increasingly apparent to me that the department was not practising what it preached and I was uncomfortable at what I saw as a hypocritical disconnect between the policy it was preaching on the one hand and its own practice on the other. I was also increasingly frustrated by the likelihood that if I stayed with the company much longer I would become type cast as a Personnel specialist for the rest of my career.

I should add, however, that I was also quite sad to leave ICI and not just because joining the Diplomatic Service (see below) meant taking a substantial drop in salary! The company had been good to me as indeed it was to all its staff. Notwithstanding my comments above the Personnel function, which included some strong characters, had for many years had a key role in setting the tone through generous salaries and allowances and through an elaborate consultation mechanism consisting of works councils at factory level in the various Divisions of the company and an annual joint consultation council chaired by ICI's Chairman and attended by the main board directors. This was typically held in a swish seaside hotel or hydro.

Chapter 6

Late Entrant

At all events a long-held ambition to enter the Diplomatic Service reasserted itself at this point. Accordingly I applied to join the Foreign and Commonwealth Officer (FCO) as what they charmingly called a 'late entrant'. Somewhat to my surprise after the usual Civil Service Selection Board (CSSB) process I found myself selected, along with five other 'late entrants', to start work in London in the spring of 1971. I can only assume that the selectors must have thought that my commercial experience with ICI might come in useful. Their decision seemed all the more surprising when I learned afterwards from a friend whose name I had given as a referee that, when asked as part of the security vetting process why he thought I wanted to join the Service, he had replied that he had no idea and thought I must be out of my mind. Certainly the starting salary, even at first secretary level, was considerably less than my salary in ICI.

So it was that I embarked rather late on a new career. It proved to be a decision which I never regretted though life would probably have been much easier for Val and the family had I remained with ICI. My first job was in a functional department called somewhat misleadingly 'Financial Policy and Aid' since it neither made financial policy nor gave any aid. My main role was to interface with the Overseas Development Ministry, as it then was, just across St James's Park. There was no special training, not even an induction course as far as I can recall. You were just expected to pick it up as you went along.

I quickly discovered that I was now part of an organisation with a very strong *esprit de corps* and a sense of being able to cope with anything the world might throw at it. Consequently expectations were high, not least in terms of the sheer volume of work which an individual could get through in the course of a day. It was also a world of tight deadlines, whether a brief to be completed in time for the Minister's box closing that evening or a set of supplementaries in time for a Parliamentary Question the following day. It was very different from the more leisurely pace of the ICI Head Office down the road at Millbank. The contrast was vividly brought home to me when towards the end of my first week in the department I came back at about 6pm from a long meeting at ODM to be greeted by my Head of Department, Peter Marshall, later Sir Peter Marshall who went on to become Deputy Secretary General of the Commonwealth. He asked me how the meeting went and I told him. He then said it would be interesting to see the record. When I replied that I would do it in the morning he said in no uncertain terms that I had better do it straight away as there would not be time in the morning.

Although the formal structure was hierarchical, I was pleasantly surprised by the easy informality which pervaded the office with most people on first name terms regardless of rank. The whole environment fostered a 'can do' spirit. By the same token the average desk officer, however inexperienced, was expected to be, or rapidly to become, an expert on the country, or policy area, for which he was responsible. Provided he did so then his recommendations could influence policy decisions both within the FCO at Ministerial level and on occasions at Cabinet level. Critics regarded this with disapproval as the cult of the amateur but in my experience it worked remarkably well.

The 'can do' spirit to which I have referred was put to the test during the miners' strike in 1972 and its aftermath which caused considerable disruption including extensive power cuts. In the following year the Heath government had to put the country on a three-day working week to conserve coal stocks. There could of course be no such thing as a three-day week in the FCO which had to keep functioning 24/7. As there was little or no electric light on the off days, staff worked in the evenings by candlelight. Likewise, as there were few or no trains running, some people stayed overnight sleeping on camp beds. During the disruption I was lucky enough to find a bed for several nights at the then Royal Commonwealth Society in Northumberland Avenue.

However, although mercifully free at that time of management jargon, I always thought that the FCO, and the Civil Service more generally, could have learned a lesson from the business world about the most effective use of resources. As I had experienced it in ICI if, for instance, a marketing manager was given a specific task or objective he would also be given the necessary resources (funding, staff etc) to carry it out. If he failed he would of course have to suffer the consequences. He might be sacked or perhaps simply moved and miss out on promotion. By contrast in the FCO, and no doubt in the rest of the Civil Service, an individual would typically be given a job to do without necessarily the resources to do it properly. In the fullness of time, perhaps after a lengthy post inspection, the deficiency might be corrected. But in the meantime the job would not be done properly and/or the individual might be chronically overworked.

As for my role, I soon realised that the ODM machine was a powerful juggernaut with an ethos and momentum of its own deriving from the early days in the sixties when it was led by Barbara Castle. The Treasury might well dictate the overall size of the aid budget but within that limit ODM was pretty free to decide how and where the money should be spent. Although we in the FCO could quote Prime Minister Edward Heath's dictum that aid should be 'a tool of foreign policy' and seek to remind the Department that it was dispensing British taxpayers' money, in practice this made little difference to the way ODM operated. Over the years a succession of Ministers were successfully 'captured' by the Department. Even when Margaret Thatcher abolished the Ministry and turned it into the Overseas Development Administration with a Minister of State answering to the Foreign Secretary, it proved difficult to persuade it to change its ways.

Shortly after Britain joined the European Economic Community, as it was then known, I was asked to represent HMG in a so-called high level group of experts from the member states on 'développement globale'. I have no idea what the remit was supposed to be but we talked endlessly around the pros and cons of food aid. I well remember one particular meeting which was chaired by a rather pompous Belgian diplomat (Belgium had the Presidency of the EC at the time). At one point the Irish delegate, who like me was a new boy on the block (Ireland and Denmark had just joined at the same time as the UK), evidently disagreed with something the chairman had said and was heard to comment 'I think that will be when the Mountains of Mourne come down to the sea.' I switched over my earphone set to hear how this quintessentially Irish remark would be rendered into French. The interpreter was clearly out of her depth and said nothing. This caused the puzzled French delegate to seek clarification directly from his Irish counterpart. After a lengthy dialogue between the two in a mixture of French and English the Frenchman, finally thinking that he had understood, said 'ah, vous voulez dire jamais' to which the Irish delegate, now equally mystified, replied 'oh no, I never said that.'

I do not know what the other members of the group made of this little exchange but for me it was both a moment to treasure and a vivid illustration of the scope for misunderstandings in multilateral diplomacy and of the need to use clear and simple language. However, at the end of the meeting, when a large bundle of paper was handed out by the chairman for each of us to take back to our capitals for further study and comment, my Irish counterpart made his position abundantly clear. 'Mr Chairman, I doubt if we have the facilities in Dublin to photocopy this lot, let alone read it.'

At that time I, like most of my FCO colleagues, thought that joining the EEC was the right thing to do in the long term interests of the UK. We were, of course, well aware of its defects – its notorious democratic deficit, and the lack of transparency and accountability at the Commission. But there was an underlying optimism, call it naive if you like, that if only we could get in then we could change things for the better. Now the majority, albeit a very small one, of the British people have concluded that we should leave which implies that we have failed in that endeavour. Arguably the seeds of failure were sown from the start not only by de Gaulle's veto but at a deeper level by the very fact that we were not in the enterprise from the very beginning and were not one of the founder members. Accordingly it was not, and was never going to be, 'our show' as the empire had been. It also did not help that, although we had signed up to the idea of ever closer union as embodied in the Treaty of Rome, this fact was never properly explained at the time to the British people either by Ted Heath or Harold Wilson.

Nevertheless, I believe that we should have stuck with it. We could I believe over time have found allies within the EU in our effort to make the whole bureaucratic affair more genuinely democratic, more transparent and more accountable. Crucially we could have led the way in making it more open to free and fair trade with the rest of the world and indeed prevented further premature moves towards some kind of political federation.

Chapter 7

A Small Town in Germany

My two-year apprenticeship in London came to an end in May 1973 when I was posted to the Embassy in Bonn and the family faced yet another change of scene. At that time Bonn was not only the capital of the then Federal Republic of Germany but also, along with Berlin, at the epicentre of the Cold War which was at its height. There had never been a peace treaty at the end of the war and as a result the position and 'rights' of the four victorious 'allies' in their respective zones of occupation remained much as they had developed in practice at the end of the war. This was fairly unsatisfactory for all concerned and an attempt was made to codify the position based on existing practice. The negotiations culminated in the Quadripartite Agreement signed between the four wartime allies in 1971. But there were still many grey areas which the Soviets were constantly trying to exploit and expand in a bid to undermine the position of the three western allies in Berlin and in Germany as a whole – '*Deutschland als ganzes*' to use the accepted terminology at the time.

In response to this salami tactic the American, British, and French governments and the Federal government in Bonn relied heavily on advice from the so-called Bonn Group of Embassy and FRG officials meeting on an almost daily basis in Bonn. My role was as deputy to the British representative in the group. The three western embassies also had a specific responsibility to manage air traffic through the three air corridors to Berlin. These could only be used by the airlines of Britain, France and the US – in those days BEA, Air France and PanAm. The embassies also oversaw the work of the three allied military governments in West Berlin.

The whole situation was fragile and chock-full of anomalies. While we had eventually recognised the German Democratic Republic (GDR), we had never accepted in principle, as distinct from practice, the division of Berlin. Consequently we could not recognise East Berlin as the capital of the GDR. Yet after the GDR was officially recognised all three western allies had set up their embassies there. The tortuous language used to get round this apparent contradiction was to say that they were embassies 'to', not 'in' the GDR. A rather ironic parallel was drawn with, for example, the recognition of the government of Free France represented by General de Gaulle in London during the war. While there were checkpoints at the crossings between East and West Berlin neither the Soviets nor the East Germans had the right to stop official cars from the British, French or US Military Governments from going into East Berlin and we made a practice of exercising the right to do so. We could not however drive out of Berlin and into the GDR proper. On one occasion Val and I drove in a British army patrol car to the very furthest suburb on the south east fringe of Berlin. At that point we were within about thirty kilometres of Val's old home in the village of Klein Köris where she had lived with her parents during the war years and which had been at the centre of the Wehrmacht's last stand before Berlin. It was a very emotional experience.

The three military governments also had the right to fly helicopters over Berlin. On one occasion on a very hot summer's day I was offered a flight in a British army helicopter. Because of the heat the pilot decided to leave the doors off. Consequently as we banked sharply to avoid entering GDR airspace, I found myself gazing out over Berlin from a height of several thousand feet with nothing holding me in other than my seat belt. As I have always been allergic to heights this was not the happiest of experiences. We also had the right, unlike ordinary folk, to travel from the FRG across GDR territory to West Berlin by approved autobahns and on the British military train which ran daily with a military escort. To make its identity quite clear the train had emlazoned in large letters on each coach *Eigentum der Britischen Rheinarmee*. When crossing the border at Helmstedt only the Soviet military police were allowed to check our passports. The GDR border police were not allowed on board.

At the same time all four wartime allies still maintained small military missions with the right to patrol widely in 'Germany as a whole' except in certain designated sensitive areas – mainly military installations. Thus the Soviet military mission could roam around the FRG and our military mission, Brixmis, could do likewise in the GDR. Of course both sides were tempted to push the boundaries and explore into the sensitive areas. As a result there were frequent minor incidents with on occasions the crews of the patrol cars being temporarily detained. Any one of these could have been escalated into a major crisis had either side chosen to do so. With hindsight it is near miraculous that none of them did spark a major confrontation.

As it was, the cat and mouse game continued and the whole fragile construct survived right up to the collapse of the GDR. I believe that the Bonn Group's highly developed expertise played a significant part in helping the Western powers to maintain a firm but appropriate response to the provocations from the Soviet Union and to minimise the risk of misunderstandings. In the process the members of the Group developed a dynamic and a jargon of their own and often found that they had more in common with each other than with their respective governments. We were all on first name terms except that the FRG delegates remained formal when speaking to each other. The French stood out as the most jealous in defence of their rights as a victorious ally.

With the Cold War still intense, Bonn and Berlin were also centres of intrigue and intelligence gathering. The Bonn Group was necessarily closely involved with the various intelligence agencies and with a variety of NATO organizations. It had become the practice to mount a secret exercise each year to practise how the four western allies in particular, and NATO as a whole, would respond to a sudden armed provocation from the Soviet Union. On one such occasion when the exercise was launched at a week-end I happened to be acting as the duty officer for the Bonn Group. The scenario was that the Soviets had sent military aircraft down one of the Berlin air corridors which were supposed to be for civilian use only. How should the West respond? My quiet afternoon was rudely interrupted when the public telephone rang in the Embassy. When I picked it up an American voice said 'this is so and so, from … (he then named a NATO organisation). We've decided to send a squadron of fighters down the central corridor to counter this Soviet threat and warn them off.' When I pointed out that he was speaking on a public line he said 'sure, but this is only an exercise and it seemed the quickest way of getting through.' He had evidently not realised that it was precisely because it was an exercise that he needed to protect the information and not least the role of the organisation from which he was speaking. It was an interesting example of how skewed people's thinking can become when they are living in such a world of subterfuge and suspicion.

The whole situation has been graphically portrayed in John Le Carré's spy novel *A Small Town In Germany* based on the time when he was serving in the Embassy in the sixties. Shortly after my arrival in Bonn in 1973 the notorious Guillaume affair erupted. Guillaume was a GDR agent who got himself employed in the office of the Federal Chancellor, Willi Brandt, where he had access to much top secret information. Shortly after Guillaume was exposed I happened to be speaking to a senior German official in a highly sensitive post. He explained over lunch that any German with the appropriate qualifications, whether from the GDR or the Federal Republic, was entitled to apply for a position in the Civil Service. Consequently, although there was a vetting process, it was extremely difficult to determine where an individual's true loyalty lay. This prompted me to ask him, rather cheekily, where he originally came from, to which he replied with an enigmatic smile and a heavily accented first syllable 'Dresden'.

It is greatly to his credit that despite all the suspicion and cold war tension Willi Brandt insisted on the need to open a dialogue with the GDR and in particular with Poland. If it did not bring any immediate results it is arguable that his Ostpolitik began a process which helped eventually to bring about the collapse of the GDR and indeed the end of the Cold War.

After two busy years I transferred to the Embassy's defence policy job focused primarily on the interface between the British forces in Germany and the FRG, and on the British military presence in Berlin. One constant irritant derived from the RAF's need to hone its low-flying capability so that if it ever came to a shooting war with the Soviet Union they could attack into enemy territory under the radar. Although the practice area was over relatively sparsely populated farm land, inevitably the noise upset the farmers and especially their cattle. Consequently there were frequent claims for compensation. With hindsight it was pretty arrogant to insist on flying over FRG territory when presumably the same result could have been achieved either out to sea or over remote areas of the UK. One other feature of the work was helping to negotiate the annual budget for the British Military Government in Berlin, the in-country costs of which were paid for by the German taxpayer. In this role I was the piggy in the middle between the demands of the military on the one hand and the understandable reluctance of the Federal German authorities on the other hand to pay more than was strictly necessary. Fortunately the latter well understood the need to provide financial support for the British military presence in Berlin which provided a critical part of the guarantee of West Berlin's survival.

One of my trickiest assignments at this time was negotiating with the Queen's advisers the finer points of Her Majesty's visit to the FRG to review her army on the occasion of her Silver Jubilee in 1977. This was not a state visit and so there was no precedent and little protocol to go by. In the event it was decided that German sensitivities could be satisfied by the Queen inviting the President of the Federal Republic to come to the review as her guest. However this involved the playing of both national anthems and I remember some heated discussion at a planning meeting in Buckingham Palace as to the order in which they should be played. The meeting was not amused when I suggested that the best solution might be to play them both simultaneously. In the event the Queen's flying visit was entirely successful. The President reciprocated the Queen's invitation by inviting Her Majesty to join him for a *vin d'honneur* at a nearby schloss.

As a result of my many contacts at this time with all ranks in BAOR and RAF Germany I came to have a high regard for their professionalism and spirit. On one occasion when visiting a tank regiment on manoeuvres on the Lüneburg Heath I asked a tank commander how he felt about the latest information to the effect that the number of Soviet tanks in central Europe outnumbered the allies by about 11 to 1. He replied, only half-joking, that each Chieftain tank carried about 50 rounds of armour piercing shells and they should of course be able to destroy at least 11 Soviet tanks with that amount of ammunition.

Overall life in the Embassy was quite tough with very long hours, often including week-ends, the norm. But it had its lighter moments as when a senior member of staff found himself locked inside the sound-proof safe speech room late one night when everyone else except the security guard had gone home. To avoid the risk of electronic detection the room was not only specially clad but also had no telephone. The only door, also heavily clad, was hermetically sealed from the inside by pulling on a long metal lever. Unfortunately on this occasion the lever snapped just as the door locked leaving the poor man trapped inside with no means of communicating with the outside world other than by wireless telegram to London. So his only option was to send a telegram to the Resident Clerk (ie duty officer) at the FCO telling of his predicament and asking the clerk to telephone the security guard to open the door from the outside. It took several increasingly desperate messages to convince the Resident Clerk that he was not the victim of an out of season April fool joke.

There were other compensations as well, not least that we were within easy reach of Val's mother in Koblenz and of her brother and his family.

The author and his father in O'Connell Street, Dublin during the war, summer holidays 1943.

The old Rectory in Omagh where I grew up. Long since demolished. (Clearly photographed in wartime as evidence by the Army Chaplain's truck)

My mother as a VAD at Great
Ormond Street Hospital,
London, in the First World War.

Leading the parade. Our daughter Fiona in Mpwawa 1960.

Pen and Sword Books
c/o Casemate Publishers
1950 Lawrence Road
Havertown, PA 19083

HISTORY BROUGHT BACK TO LIFE WITH PEN & SWORD BOOKS

Pen & Sword Books have over 6000 books currently available and we cover all periods of history on land, sea and air.

If you would like to hear more about our other titles sign up now and receive 30% off your next purchase. www.penandswordbooks.com/newsletter/

By signing up to our free discounts, reviews on new releases, previews of forthcoming titles and upcoming competitions, so you will never miss out!

Not online? Return this card to us with your contact details and we will put you on our catalog mailing list.

Mr/Mrs/Ms ....

Address...

Zip Code.......................... Email address..

Website: www.penandswordbooks.com
Email: Uspen-and-sword@casematepublishers.com · Telephone: (610) 853-9131
Stay in touch: facebook.com/penandswordbooks or follow us on Twitter @penswordbooks

We hope you enjoyed this book!

Tanganyika Reunion 2008, fifty years on. All of us had sailed out together on the SS Kenya Castle to Dar es Salaam in August 1958. We were all DO (Cadets) on first appointment.

The staff in our bungalow at the High Commission, New Delhi. 'The heroes' as we called them.

With Mrs. Gandhi after she had signed the condolence book in the High Commission on the death of Earl Mountbatten.

Tidbinbilla space tracking station, Canberra where our late friend Tom Reid, the Director, was the first person on earth to hear Neil Armstrong's 'small step for man …'.

With Lynda Chalker at President Museveni's camp in eastern Uganda.

Visiting Museveni's ranch at Rwakitura.

Meeting Pope John Paul II on his visit to Uganda in June 1993.

The Residence, Kampala. Dressed overall for the Queen's Birthday.

Val with the Residence team, Kampala.

With KAR veterans of World War II at the Residence, Kampala.

HRH The Prince of Wales at OSPA's farewell event, 8 June 2017.

The team at OSPA's farewell in London. From left David Le Breton's daughter, David's wife Patricia, David Le Breton, secretary and key player, Alison Hamilton, David's PA, Val, our daughter Fiona and me.

We were also fortunate in having delightful German neighbours, Ulli and Renate Weisgerber with whom we shared several memorable wine tastings in the upper reaches of the Moselle and along the rivers Saar and Ruwer. Ulli had been conscripted as a teenager towards the end of the war and sent to Yugoslavia. As the war ended he managed to escape from the partisans and walked back across the mountains into Austria where he gave himself up to a British army patrol. By the time we knew him he had become a prominent and much respected paediatrician. The next house to ours, on the other side, was the residence of the Jamaican Ambassador and his fun-loving family with whom we became good friends.

There were, however, quite strict rules applied by the local Council about what one could and could not do, for example, with garden waste. For one thing burning of autumn leaves, as then practised in the UK, was not allowed. This caused us a problem as we had a number of plane trees in and around our garden which shed copious leaves the size of dinner plates. How to dispose of them? When I rang the local authority to ask for advice they told me that they should be collected into plastic bags and lined up on the pavement outside the house from where they would be collected by the Council. As both Val and I were particularly busy at the time and we had no gardener it was a few weeks before we were able to collect the leaves and line them up. However nothing happened. Our orderly line up of plastic bags remained untouched on the pavement for day after day. When I rang up to ask what was happening I was told rather peremptorily that 'the leaf collecting time is over.' Eventually in desperation we took advantage of a windy night to scatter the leaves down the road. Not very neighbourly perhaps but nobody complained.

Bonn itself was plumply comfortable if a bit dull. It had been chosen by Konrad Adenauer to serve as the capital of the FRG partly because it was convenient to his own home, was fairly central between north and south Germany, and perhaps most importantly to make the point that it was a temporary expedient which could never replace Berlin as the ultimate capital of a reunified Germany. Its temporary status was reflected in the under-stated, utilitarian style of the various embassies, none more so than the British which looked more like a box factory than an Embassy. It also had the unusual distinction of facing the main road the wrong way apparently because the planners in Whitehall forgot that it is customary on the continent to drive on the right.

The Germans had a saying that in Bonn either it is raining, or the level crossing gates are shut, or both. The Americans' rather more cruel take was that Bonn was half the size of the Chicago cemetery and twice as dead. The climate could be quite oppressively heavy and humid especially in summer and there was a rumour that the Kaiser had routinely sent his Schutztruppe to Bonn for acclimatisation before they were despatched to Germany's African colonies. Whether true or not the German population, particularly the many civil servants and their families who were not from the area, had convinced themselves that the climate was so unhealthy as to cause numerous cases of *Kreislaufstörungen* (ie circulatory problems) which in turn needed to be treated by sending the patient on a *kur* to a spa resort. Eventually some of the Embassy wives, fearing that they too might be suffering from the same affliction, decided that it was time to get some medical advice from a British source. Accordingly an RAF doctor from the nearby base at Wegberg was invited to come and meet them. Unfortunately the invitation got garbled in transmission and he came to the meeting thinking that the ladies wanted to hear him speak about the problem of obesity. When told that they actually wanted to discuss the problem of Kreislaufstörungen his diagnosis was simple and direct. 'As I see it', said he in a broad Glaswegian accent, 'this is all about circulation of the blood and the answer is that either you have it, in which case you'r all reet, or you haven't in which case your deed.' There was no more talk of circulatory problems after that.

Nevertheless, notwithstanding the climate, Bonn was an excellent base for exploring the beauty and rich history of the Rhineland and the surrounding countryside on those rare occasion when we could get away. Professionally there was the satisfaction of knowing that we were at the coal face in the Cold War, and the pleasure of working with agreeable and highly able colleagues both in the embassy and among our German, US and French counterparts. There was also plenty of stimulating inter-action with senior officers in BAOR and RAF Germany. Although at the time Britain's economic woes had led to it being labelled 'the sick man of Europe' the Embassy managed to maintain an up-beat image of the country. This was due in large part to the superb leadership provided by our Ambassador Nicko Henderson and his successor Oliver Wright. Both in their different ways represented Britain with great skill, energy and panache.

Towards the end of our time in Bonn we had the remarkable good fortune to almost stumble on our present home in the village of Bidborough near

Tunbridge Wells in Kent. During a short spell of leave back in the UK we had been looking in a desultory way for a house further out in the country than our then current suburban house in Beckenham to serve as a base from then on for us and for the family. I say good fortune for three reasons. First, the house itself is a lovely family home with some splendid early nineteenth century features and magnificent views. Secondly we were able to buy it for a song because nobody at that time was interested in a large house and the couple who owned it were splitting up and anxious to dispose of it quickly. Thirdly, we found ourselves in the middle of a lively and friendly community, both then and since.

Chapter 8

India

After a spell back in London I was lucky enough to be granted my request for a posting to India. Ever since Val and I had spent a few days in Delhi during home leave from Kuala Lumpur we both had an ambition to return and find out more about the country and the sub continent which is so different from everywhere else on earth. In my case I suppose there was also a sub-conscious wish to know more of the land where my mother had been born, my grandfather and my uncle had served, and my grandmother had died at the age of barely 21.

The contrast between the ordered and regulated life of Bonn and the chaos of India with its crowds, noise, smells and colour could not have been more stark. Nearly every day was full of interest and brought something new and different, and we quickly learned to expect the unexpected. As Head of Chancery at the High Commission in Delhi it was our lot to be housed in a modern bungalow on the huge compound which was home to several hundred people including many local staff and the ex-Gurkha chowkidars. The compound was self-contained with its own little restaurant, swimming pool, tennis court and even a five bed hospital with a UK doctor. In short it was a kind of mini Surbiton in the middle of Delhi. Some of the junior staff hardly ever left its comfortable security. But for us it had the serious disadvantage of cutting us off from easy contact with Indians. While we could visit them freely they had to pass through security at the main entrance to the compound in order to visit us. It was our pleasure that so many of them chose to do so.

My posting got off to an inauspicious start when I had a bout of laryngitis and lost my voice completely the day before I was due to fly out from the UK. Clearly there would be little point in arriving in a new post unable to speak. So at the very last moment I had to ring up from home and try to explain in a hoarse whisper what had happened (there was no such thing as email or text messages in those days). Fortunately the High Commissioner,

Sir John Thomson, was very understanding and my posting was delayed by a few days.

I eventually arrived a few weeks ahead of Val who was teaching at the time and needed to see out the term. It was quickly borne in upon me that the five Indian staff we had inherited in the bungalow were in charge of me, not the other way round. They were completely set in their ways and in their respective roles which reflected the castes they came from. We had a head bearer, Shri Ram (lit. Mr God), a cook, a second bearer, a mali (gardener) and a sweeper. Both Shri Ram and the second bearer had smart uniforms with resplendent white pugarees.

The ménage worked well enough as long as one did not try to change anything. However at first I had not properly understood this. Thus, having noticed that the sweeper was simply moving the dust from one corner of the room to another, I got down on hands and knees to show him how to collect it with a dustpan and brush. This caused Shri Ram to prostrate himself in horror on the floor lower than me as it was unthinkable that the sahib should lower himself to the same level as the sweeper. There was nothing for it but to give up the attempt. On another occasion around the middle of March I was astonished to see the mali pulling out all the flowers and, worse still, the vegetables and throwing them away. When I told him to stop he refused point blank explaining that mid-March was the end of the cool season and nothing could be grown after that. Later on, after Val had arrived, she managed to persuade him, and the other house staff, to be a bit more flexible in their ways.

We had a vivid illustration one day of the pervasiveness of the caste system even though it had long been made technically illegal. We decided to give the sweeper an opportunity to better himself by dressing him in a smart uniform and asking him to help out as a bearer at a smart buffet supper we were giving for a number of Indian friends and contacts. Although it was not apparent to us that he looked any different from any other bearers we were warned afterwards by our friends that we should not do this again or we would find that people no longer accepted our invitations. No doubt attitudes may have softened since then but at least in the rural areas caste is still a major factor.

Another early challenge was learning the art of driving in India. Elsewhere in the world driving is a skill to be acquired; in India it is, or certainly was, more of an art which the westerner can only aspire to imitate. The first essential is to give way to other vehicles that are bigger than you whoever theoretically has right of way. You should include in the definition of vehicles that are bigger than you elephants, camel carts and bullock carts. Conversely you should not give way to any vehicle smaller than you. If you do you will merely cause confusion or possibly an accident. Secondly, if somewhat confusingly, you should be prepared for the other driver to do whatever you would least expect. You can console yourself with the thought that he will expect the same of you. Hence, for example, last minute turns across the traffic with no signal do not normally cause an accident while elsewhere they well might. Lastly you needed to recognise that it is a basic right of all drivers in India to drive in the middle of the road. This meant that no matter how wide the road may be, and some of the roads in New Delhi are very wide, it was always liable to be congested in the middle. Of course nowadays it is quite simply congested right across its width, however wide it may be.

At the same time you could puzzle over and enjoy the unique turn of phrase on Indian road signs which I made a point of collecting. Among my favourites were, on approaching a corner, 'Better late than…', and, after you have gone round the corner fully expecting to see the rest of the sign saying 'never', a new sign appears saying simply '…later'. Another one over a garage was 'tinkering 24 hours a week'. One sign on the approach to a single lane bridge over the Beas river in the foothills of the Himalayas read 'Delay causes frust rations(sic). Avoid it'. How you could avoid it, as there was a red light at the entrance to the bridge, was never explained. Another sign we came across more recently on a return visit to Delhi was ' Delhi Police. With you for always', prominently displayed on the side of police patrol cars – a wonderful combination of promise and threat.

India could also claim the credit, if that is the right word, for inventing the concept of 'just in time' well before it was developed as a management tool. On a number of occasions I marvelled at the ability of Indians to improvise when things went wrong at the last minute or had not been properly planned in advance. I recall in particular one example at Delhi airport when the President of Cyprus was arriving on a state visit – one of many Heads of State who came to call after Mrs Gandhi was re-elected as Prime Minister. Just as his plane touched down it was noted that the Cypriot flag was flying upside down over the saluting dais. This was easy to spot as the flag is basically a map of the island. There was clearly not going to be enough time to haul it down and hoist it back up again before the guest arrived at the podium above which it was flying. In a trice an athletic young man (I know not who) had shinned up the pole and somehow lifted the flag off the top and turned it round the right way just before the honoured guest arrived underneath it.

As time went on, despite the drawback of living on the compound, we developed a wide circle of Indian contacts, many of whom became friends. I shall always remember their warm hospitality. Happily we are still in touch with some of them to this day. With memories of the Raj still fresh in the minds of the older generation, Indian attitudes toward Britain were divided between those who looked upon the country through rose-tinted spectacles and others for whom Britain was seen much more negatively as the former occupying power. On the whole younger people were more detached. With the passage of time since the early eighties I believe that both attitudes have softened and we are left with many special ties including the English language, a common legal inheritance, and a fundamental belief in democracy as the fairest, if not the most efficient, form of government. These tangible consequences of the Raj are complemented and reinforced by the large and vibrant immigrant community from India who have made such a huge and positive contribution to life in Britain.

The closeness of the ties between our two countries was vividly illustrated by the widespread reaction in India to the news of the assassination of Earl Mountbatten by the IRA in 1979. Not only did the Morarji Desai government declare three days of national mourning but many of the leading members of it, including the President of India, attended the memorial service in Westminster Abbey. There was also a special memorial service in Delhi cathedral and many leading figures in public life in India came to sign the condolence book at the High Commission. In the absence of the High Commissioner it fell to me to receive Indira Gandhi when she called in to sign the book. I was struck by how animated, but also how tiny, she was.

Part of the fascination of India was, and still is, its unpredictability and its capacity to produce the unexpected and make it seem like the norm. There was also the warmth and refreshing eccentricity of its people and the colour and vibrancy of Indian festivals from the camel fair at Pushkar to the excitement of diwali and the kumbh mela. Every year we had the pleasure of attending the huge and colourful Republic Day parade on 15 January along the magnificent Rajpath in the centre of New Delhi. This was an extraordinary and eccentric mix of marching troops, military hardware, elephants, camels, and folk pageants and dancers from the different states of the Union. For me the climax of the celebrations was the ceremony of beating retreat performed immaculately by the massed pipes and drums of the Gurkha regiments of the Indian army as the sun set behind the red sandstone of Lutyen's Presidential Palace. Nearly twenty years after his death the bands still ended the ceremony with the haunting tune of 'Abide With Me' which had been one of Nehru's favourites.

We had the privilege of being free to travel almost anywhere in the sub continent and Val and I took full advantage of this whenever I could get away. Val also travelled widely with Indian and expatriate friends. On one occasion they arranged to hire for a week a complete carriage comprising sleeping berths, sitting and dining room, kitchen and bathroom all resplendent in wood panelling, brass fittings and velvet cushions. The carriage dated back to the Raj and had been used by judges on circuit. Val and her friends spent much time in the month beforehand negotiating the terms of the hire with a gentleman who enjoyed the splendid title of Controller of the Northern Railway. The deal was that their carriage would be hooked on to regular services in Rajasthan and shunted into sidings in the places they wished to visit such as Jaipur, Bikaner and Jodhpur. To avoid being shaken about at the back of the train it was even agreed that the carriage would be placed in the middle which of course meant that each train had to be broken up every time the carriage was to be unhooked, or hooked on again. To complete the deal they had on board with them not only a cook but also an electrician, presumably in case they might need to change a light bulb! Such an arrangement could only ever have happened in India and sadly would not be imaginable today.

On another occasion through one of our Indian connections we arranged to hire a former hunting lodge of the Maharajah near Pahalgam in Kashmir. From there we set out with both Fiona and Robert on a trek into the Himalayas which included camping at about 13,000 feet in country where black bears were flourishing as there was a ban on hunting them. Our band of guides kept them at bay overnight by maintaining a large fire in front of the cave where the guides slept. But we spent a sleepless night listening to the snuffling of the bears outside our rather flimsy tent. The views on the trek were spectacular but it was quite a relief to get back down to the valley several days later, not least because I have never had a good head for heights. While staying in the hunting lodge we had at first been puzzled by the absence of people during the day even though there was a village nearby surrounded by corn fields. However we soon found the reason. The villagers had to sit up all night on the flat roofs of their dwellings banging pots and pans to keep bears away from the ripening corn to which the bears were extremely partial. Consequently when daylight came and the bears wandered away the villagers were at last able to go to sleep.

On another safari,while staying overnight in a modest hotel in Jaipur, we were woken up by screams coming from the neighbouring bedroom. When we went to investigate we found that a lady guest had woken up to find her toes being nibbled by a rat. Understandably she was in quite a state. I ran downstairs to the reception desk only to find nobody there. But there was a large vulture perched on the desk beside the only telephone. Fortunately the manager then materialised from somewhere and phoned for a doctor. When I asked him afterwards about the vulture he said in a matter of fact way that it had a broken wing and came in every evening for shelter. After that it seemed superfluous to ask about the rats.

On another day when calling on an official in the Foreign Ministry I was heading towards his office along a wide corridor in the magnificent secretariat building when I noticed a monkey drinking out of a cup. Although I was used to seeing monkeys in unexpected places in New Delhi I had not previously seen one drinking out of a cup. When I remarked on this to the messenger who was accompanying me he replied in a matter of fact way that the monkey had a headache so they had given it a cup of tea. Ah well. Perhaps he was just joking.

Still in Delhi Val and I had a surprise invitation from a Sikh gentleman whom we had previously met at a wedding. He was the President of a farming cooperative and a leading light in the Sikh community. We were invited to attend as his guests an event which the community was organising to mark the two hundredth anniversary of the birth of the great Sikh hero Ranjit Singh. We knew it was to be in the newly opened sports arena for the Asian games and assumed we would watch a spectacle of some sort. Perhaps we should have realised that something more might be involved by the wording on the invitation which was addressed to 'His Most Benign Excellency'. In the event we found ourselves welcomed centre stage, garlanded profusely, and it was then made clear that I was expected to address the crowd who must have numbered at least five thousand. Fortunately adrenalin kicked in, helped by the fact that we had just returned from a visit to the Sikhs' holiest shrine, the Golden Temple in Amritsar. I managed to start by greeting the crowd with the only Punjabi phrase I knew followed by a reference to our visit to the Golden Temple. After that whatever I said was received with loud applause. But it was a salutary reminder of the truth of the old advice never to make assumptions.

During our time in India I had an opportunity to make an official visit to Bangalore, the booming capital of the state of Karnataka. At the end of the visit Val and I had a few hours to spare before our flight back to Delhi. I knew that my mother had been born there and that her mother had died there three years later. It occurred to me that I should try to find my grandmother's grave but I had no idea where it might be or indeed if it still existed. Although it seemed a very long shot Val and I took ourselves to the Anglican cathedral where, serendipitously, we found an elderly Anglo-Indian lady in the vestry. After I had told her my grandmother's name and the approximate year of her death the old lady hauled down a dusty tome from the top of a cupboard and within a few moments, to my great surprise, she had found a record of my grandmother's death and that she had died of dysentery, like so many of that generation before the development of intravenous drips. The record did not state where my grandmother was buried. However, having found out from me that my grandfather had been in the Indian army, the lady told us that the grave would probably be in the old British military cemetery on the Rosa road. With the light fading we hurriedly set off in a 'tuktuk' and within minutes had found my grandmother's grave still in good condition in the middle of a large cemetery laid out in straight lines and in chronological order. The whole cemetery was being faithfully maintained by a group of local volunteers. I recognised the grave from afar because it had on it in large letters the word 'Duddie' and I remembered that my mother had told me that this was her mother's nickname. It was a very moving experience. On a later visit to India a few years ago we were saddened to see that the cemetery was now overgrown and the grave no longer visible.

Apart from a heavy entertaining schedule, Val, who had learned some Hindi, involved herself in a variety of activities which in a normal life would have been full time occupations in themselves. She regularly helped out an elderly Indian doctor, Dr Tandon, who ran an open air health clinic in a slum district of Delhi. As he could not see very well to read labels, one of her priorities was to ensure that he was giving the medication he had actually intended to his patients. She also helped out in a leprosy centre, and she was a regular visitor to Mother Teresa's home for the dying in Delhi where on more than one occasion she persuaded the nuns that an injured person was not in fact dying and urgently needed to be taken to hospital. With hindsight I marvel at the way she drove herself around Old Delhi in our ancient Land Rover. On one occasion she came upon a man lying on the side of the road with both his legs in splints. Apparently he had broken his legs in an accident and had been taken to a hospital which had set them and then discharged him on to the street. As he had no relatives in Delhi he was trying to get back to his home in Kerala. Since he could not walk Val somehow got him into the back of the Land Rover and took him to the station where she bought him a ticket back home. His long journey cannot have been easy but hopefully he got there safely.

Professionally there was never a dull moment. The High Commission had an inescapably prominent role in the diplomatic world in Delhi and there were frequent high level visits in both directions between the UK and India. During my time we had, among others, a visit by the then Foreign Secretary David Owen and then, after the Conservatives won the election in 1979, by his successor Lord Carrington and subsequently by Margaret Thatcher. This was shortly after Mrs G, as she was widely known, had won a landslide victory in an 18-day whistle-stop campaign up and down the country during which, as she later told us, she had averaged about two hours sleep a night and had personally addressed millions of people every day. Such phenomenal staying power can only be wondered at.

It is perhaps not surprising that these two formidable ladies got on well. The focal point of the Prime Minister's visit was a lengthy meeting with no officials present on either side. It would be fascinating to be able to compare the subsequent accounts of that meeting which they each gave to their respective advisers. I have an abiding memory of Mrs Thatcher being genuinely concerned about the welfare of her own and the High Commission staff because of the long hours they were having to work during her stay.

There were many other visitors too, both official and unofficial. One such was the former Prime Minister Jim Callaghan. With typical Indian hospitality he was invited as an honoured guest to stay at Rashtrapati Bhavan, the Presidential Palace. He told us how Lord Mountbatten, when staying there years after Indian independence, had noticed that nothing in the Palace had changed except that some of the pictures had been re-arranged.

At about this time we also had a visit by a senior Foreign Office official, Hugh Cortazzi, who decided that he would come in overland from Pakistan which he had also been visiting. His intention was to get a bit of the flavour of the country, or at least of the states of Punjab and Haryana, by driving through them rather than flying over them before arriving in Delhi. I went up to meet him at Wagah, the only official crossing point between the two countries. He was also greeted by a delegation from the Punjab state government and a raft of photographers as it was rare indeed for an official visitor to arrive in India by this route. As he stepped across the line from Pakistan into India he was greeted in the usual way with garlands of marigolds, and simultaneously photographed. However the cameras were pointing into Pakistan and consequently the official photographs show a smiling and heavily garlanded Hugh Cortazzi under a banner across the road reading 'Welcome to Pakistan'!

One of the highlights of our time in India was in 1981 when the Prince of Wales made an official visit which lasted for thirteen days. He flew in an aircraft of the Queen's Flight of which on several occasions he took control. He made a very favourable impression on people wherever he went, not least by his remarkable memory for people and faces and by his evident enthusiasm for India. I had the good fortune to be asked to reconnoitre in advance a suitable location where he could escape for a day or two to relax away from his gruelling programme which included over a hundred events. This was the justification for a visit which Val and I made to Kanha tiger reserve deep in the forest in Maharashtra which reputedly had been the inspiration for Kipling's Jungle Book. During the visit we spent two memorable nights in an old forest department guest house from the days of the Raj with a long thatched roof, and complete with a punkah, though unfortunately no punkah wallah, and the old crested china. We heard, but never saw, a tiger though we had spent a nervous few hours waiting for it to return to the remains of a kill which it had made the previous day. In the event it was decided that the location was just too remote and that its rudimentary landing strip was not safe enough to be used by the Prince's aircraft. But the nervous barking of the chital deer in the stillness of the night will remain with me for ever.

In those days there were many gangs of robbers, locally known as dacoits, roaming the countryside. On the long drive back from Kanha to Delhi, somewhere near the Chambal river, we were stopped on a lonely stretch of road by a gang of dacoits, clearly intent on robbing us. Fortunately we had with us a formidable English lady who had spent most of her life in India. With remarkable courage she jumped out of the Range Rover and ran at the gang hurling obscene abuse at them in Hindi. They were so taken aback by this apparition that they froze for long enough to enable us to drive through. Not long after this incident Val was travelling back on her own from a visit to Calcutta on the Rajdhani express when it was stopped by another gang of dacoits who rampaged through it smashing windows and robbing the female passengers of their jewellery. Again she was lucky in that they gave up when confronted by the conductor at the entrance to the coach she was in and by a number of male passengers she had encouraged to stand up to them. Perhaps they also thought that they had been on the train for long enough and that by then the police might be about to arrive. On the whole these gangs were not a threat to life and limb. They were more akin to Robin Hood and his merry men, though maybe not so merry.

Shortly after I arrived at the High Commission we were faced with a major and wholly unforeseen immigration row when an Indian woman flying in to Heathrow was strip-searched and examined by a (female) doctor to see whether she was a virgin. She was purportedly coming to the UK as the bride of an Indian man already in Britain. There were at the time a large number of false marriages arranged solely to enable the woman to obtain the right to remain. Once granted the right to remain the man and woman simply parted company. In its efforts to reduce this inflow the Home Office seized on the theory that no self-respecting Indian man would genuinely marry a woman who was not a virgin. According to this theory if she was not a virgin the marriage must be a false one, 'arranged' indeed but not the kind of arranged marriage normally associated with India, and she should not be allowed in.

At all events when the news of the incident broke there was an outcry across India and crowds marched on the High Commission waving placards with demands to 'castrate the Heathrow rapists'. Although we issued an immediate apology this was clearly not enough and eventually David Owen had to fly out to try to calm things down. I recall one meeting with a group of irate Indian politicians at which the Foreign Secretary suggested that perhaps it was a bit inconsistent for India to make such a fuss about one isolated incident for which we had apologised and had promised that it would never happen again, while saying nothing whatever about the far greater infringement of human rights on a daily basis in the gulags of the Soviet Union with which India had a close relationship. The response was immediate and emphatic. There was no expectation that the Soviet Union would behave better. On the other hand there was an expectation that the British would behave like gentlemen, and genuine shock when they failed to do so.

Not long afterwards we were alerted to a threat from a Japanese-based terrorist organisation, the Red Army faction, who were reported to be planning an attack on a diplomatic mission in Delhi. We decided that we should take the threat seriously and at least look as though we had strengthened our security measures. Consequently I issued an instruction to our ex-Gurkha security guards, who manned the main entrance to the High Commission compound, that they should stop and search any vehicle coming in if they were not quite sure of the identity of the passengers. Unfortunately this instruction was too unclear and resulted in no action being taken. So I decided that I had better keep it simple and followed up with an instruction to search all vehicles. As it happened the very first vehicle to reach the gate after the chowkidars got this fresh order was the High Commissioner's Rolls leaving the compound with the High Commissioner in it. Undeterred by this our splendid Gurkhas nevertheless stopped it and asked the High Commissioner to get out so that it could be thoroughly searched. Fortunately for me Sir John thought it highly amusing.

The next largely unforeseen event was of an entirely different order of magnitude – the Soviet invasion of Afghanistan on Boxing Day 1979. This changed the whole scenario and introduced an element of instability into the whole region which has persisted to this day even though the Soviets, as they then were, have long since gone. We very soon found ourselves, along with the Americans, supporting the mujahideen and a number of meetings with mujahideen leaders took place at the High Commission. At the same time we were proactively engaged with the Indian government to persuade them both to use their influence in Moscow to get the Soviet Union to withdraw and simultaneously to take the opportunity to mend fences with Pakistan. I remember one particular conversation I had with a senior official in the MFA responsible for relations with western Europe in which I had suggested that it was regrettable that India had not made any public statement criticising the USSR's unprovoked invasion of a sovereign state. He replied that if your friend has his hand trapped under a boulder it does not help him if you then start hitting the boulder with a sledgehammer. Meanwhile India would continue to do what it could behind the scenes. Whether true or not I had to admit that his response was pretty clever and in the best Brahminical tradition.

Some time later I went to Islamabad on an official visit and Val and I seized the opportunity to drive up to Peshawar and through the Khyber pass to Torkham, the border crossing point into Afghanistan, having signed a book absolving the Pakistan government from any responsibility for our safety. The crossing point was a highly sensitive area and was heavily guarded by a Pakistani border force. We could not go into Afghanistan but Val was keen to at least have a photographic record of our visit. So she persuaded some of the guards to pose for the camera in their smart uniforms with their backs to the crossing point. Consequently she was able to take several shots of the landscape on the Afghan side of the border. We also visited Daraa in the tribal territory which was doing a thriving business in drugs and small arrms. In the main street lined with stalls we were offered a home made Kalashnikov for the equivalent of about £50 or the real thing for rather more. I shall never forget the sight of potential customers trying out the rifles they were about to purchase by firing them live into the air. With hindsight it was probably irresponsible on our part to go there, but it was certainly revealing.

Towards the end of my tour in Delhi one of our major preoccupations was lobbying the Indian government to support our position on the Falkland Islands in the UN. Although they did not condone the Argentine invasion of the islands they were less than enthusiastic about supporting us – why were we making such a fuss about a couple of small islands which were in any case so much nearer to Argentina than to the UK? In response I asked my Indian interlocutors how they would react if Indonesia invaded the Indian owned Banaban islands which are much nearer to Sumatra than to India. I like to think that at least this gave them pause for thought.

Notwithstanding the fact that we were at war with Argentina over the Falkland Islands there was still room for human compassion and common sense to prevail. It so happened that a female member of the Argentine Embassy staff was seriously ill as a result of a botched operation in an Indian hospital and needed a further emergency operation. At the Embassy's request we admitted her to the High Commission hospital on the compound where an emergency operation was successfully carried out and her life was saved.

Commercially there was not much scope for investment from the UK because India at the time was running a virtually closed, command economy. But there was plenty of opportunity for exports especially in defence sales where, for example, we concluded a sale to the Indian air force of some 150 Anglo-French Jaguar fighters, one of the biggest defence sales the UK had made up to then. The package included pilot training and the assembly of some of the aircraft in Bangalore. In a bizarre episode, our Air Adviser at the High Commission was asked by the Indian Air Force if he could help them to persuade the Indian customs officials in Bombay to allow them to take delivery, without paying duty, of a number of crates containing avionic parts for the Jaguars being assembled in Bangalore. When it came to selling the avionics to go into the aircraft we found ourselves at a serious disadvantage *vis á vis* the French. While they were able to promote the product of a specific French company over its other French competitors London would not allow us to do the same for any specific UK company over its UK competitors. This not only drove the Indians to distraction but I believe ended up losing us valuable business.

India was also in the process of building up a blue water navy. As part of the process she had agreed to buy the Royal Navy's flagship aircraft carrier HMS *Hermes* which was about to be retired. However, just before the deal went through the Falklands war broke out and the sale had to be hurriedly postponed. Had the outbreak happened a few weeks later *Hermes* would already have been handed-over. It is hard to see how the task force could have succeeded in re-taking the islands without her and the aircraft she carried. In the event the deal still went through after the war and *Hermes* had a new lease of life as INS *Vikrant*.

The High Commission was also overseeing the UK's largest bilateral aid programme anywhere in the world though it was just a drop in the ocean in relation to the size of the population and the economy even at that time. In *per capita* terms it was far smaller than our aid to many other countries, notably in Africa. I was not directly involved with its administration but was far from convinced of its effectiveness as a soft tool of foreign policy as earlier envisaged by Ted Heath. There is no evidence that it played any part in influencing Indian government policy towards the UK either then or since.

We left India towards the end of 1982 with mixed emotions. I treasure the memory of working under the dynamic and inspiring leadership of Sir John

Thomson. He had among other characteristics a virtually insatiable work ethic. Apart from his many activities representing a country which was still a key player in India, he also wrote extensively back to the FCO with practical suggestions for preventing the spread of nuclear weapons not only to India but more widely. I believe his work ethic was partly driven by his belief that we all of us only use a tiny percentage of our available brain power and that it would make a huge difference if we could just tap into a further one or two per cent. Unfortunately he did sometimes forget that the rest of us did not necessarily have the same motivation! That said, he was by no means a martinet and, when reminded, would readily recognise that others needed to be able to go home even if he was still at his desk.

We were both conscious that we had been very privileged to have been given an insight into a country with, along with China, the richest, oldest and most complex culture in the world. At the time India's economic development was held back by the prevalent socialist model inherited from Jawaharlal Nehru of a command economy sheltered from the outside world by high tariffs and a mass of regulations. It was fashionable in some circles in the West to look at the widespread poverty, corruption and bureaucratic inertia and write India off as a hopeless case. Happily this was not the view in the FCO or in the High Commission where Sir John Thomson's informed enthusiasm for India and optimism about its future was infectious. I need hardly add that Val and I both thought the same given all the evidence we had from our friends and contacts, and from our own experiences, of the strength and dynamism of Indian society.

Consequently it has come as no surprise to us that in the past few years India's economic development has been dramatic, especially in the field of information technology and high tech engineering, as the economy has been liberalised. India, along with China, has been largely responsible for one of the key millennium development goals to reduce world poverty being met. This has in my view had very little to do with aid despite the claims of the aid industry. Meanwhile we treasure the many friendships we made in India and welcome its increasing political and economic importance. We in the West have a vested interest in the success of India as the world's largest democracy.

Chapter 9

Australia

At the end of 1982 we found ourselves in Canberra where I had been appointed Deputy High Commissioner to Australia. It took us a while to adjust to a totally different world. We had left a densely populated and poor subcontinent with one of the world's richest and most ancient cultures and had arrived in a much larger, sparsely populated and affluent subcontinent with a far younger, essentially British-Irish culture and the remnants of a very early aborigine one.

On reaching Canberra we were struck by the sense of space, the absence of people and noise and the beauty of the surrounding countryside. The smokey blue backdrop of the Brindabellas in the middle distance reminded me of the Mountains of Mourne though on a grander scale. Our accommodation was a large 1950s-style house with a flat roof and yellow stucco walls in the fashionable inner suburb of Forrest. It was comfortable but ugly – so much so that it was known locally as the Odeon.

One drawback was the eccentric, not to say hopelessly inefficient, heating system. This consisted of an enormous gas guzzling boiler in the cellar pumping hot air up through ducts in the flooring at ground level and then through tiny ventilators in the ceilings of the bedrooms. As any school child knows, hot air rises, which meant that the only way of reaching it in the bedrooms was by standing on a chair, lifting your arms heavenwards towards the ceiling, and rubbing your hands together. This mattered because Canberra can be seriously cold in winter with the temperature on occasions dropping below freezing at night. We never discovered who was responsible for installing such an eccentric system.

As in Bonn we were again lucky with our next-door neighbours, John and June Hehir. John was a highly regarded obstetrician whose reputation among Canberra wives and their husbands was such that on one occasion when he let it be known well in advance that he intended to take a three-month sabbatical the number of births in the relevant three-month period fell sharply.

Like all self-respecting suburban houses in Canberra ours had a nature strip to the front with no fences or hedges to separate it from the neighbours' houses. While this arrangement encouraged good neighbourliness it also had its disadvantages. Thus on one occasion when the Hehirs were having a posh Sunday afternoon tea party they and their guests were somewhat surprised to see Val and me getting out of the car next door with Val wrapped in a small tablecloth and me even more inadequately clad in a copy of the *Sydney Morning Herald* as we scampered for cover in the house.

The reason for this spectacle was that early that morning we had set out with some friends from the Australian National University to climb Mt. Booth in the nearby Gudgenby National Park. Unfortunately we ran into heavy rain and thick mist on the mountain accompanied by a sudden fall in temperature. Wearing only bush shorts and shirts we were soon soaked to the skin and shivering with cold. To make matters worse we had difficulty finding our way back to the cars through the thick mist. When we did eventually get to the car our one thought was to dry out and warm up as quickly as possible. The only way to do this was to strip off our soaking garments, turn on the car's heater and head for home. We had no spare clothes with us nor even a towel. So Val made do with the tablecloth she had brought for our now aborted picnic which left only the pages of the said *Sydney Morning Herald* for me to put on as best I could. It was then our double misfortune to be stopped on the road back to Canberra by the only police road block we ever encountered during our entire stay in Australia. When they realised our predicament the police cheerfully waved us through but I shudder to think how the incident would have been reported back to base.

A year or two later we had another encounter of a different kind with members of the New South Wales police force. We had been invited to attend a special Italian dinner and ball organised by the local Returned Servicemen's League in the small town of Leeton in the Riverina district of New South Wales. The festivities went on well into the wee hours and we found on retuning to our hotel, the only one in town, that it was locked, bolted and barred. Despite all our attempts at ringing the bell and hammering on the door there was no response. As the prospect of spending a rather chilly night in the car did not appeal we decided to see if the local police might be willing to offer us sanctuary for the night in a police cell. So, clad in evening dress with Val in a full length ball gown, we made our way along the sleeping main street and up a steep rise towards the police station at the top of the rise. The building looked just like the sheriff's office in a typical Hollywood western and the door overlooking the verandah and the town was wide open. Inside were two burly police officers behind an enormous desk. The look on their faces as we climbed up the steps to the verandah was memorable. However when we explained the situation to them they immediately, and with evident relish, rang the hotel's duty manager, who lived some miles away, and told him in no uncertain terms to come in and open up the hotel. Some minutes later he arrived in a dressing gown and pyjamas and, with grateful thanks to the police, we were able to go to bed.

We soon discovered that diplomatic and social life in Canberra was considerably more formal than in Delhi. Entertaining was mainly in the form of dinner parties rather than buffet suppers as in Delhi. It was the done thing for men to wear dark suits and white shirts and you were certainly expected to arrive on time – again unlike Delhi where 'Indian standard time' was hugely elastic and it was quite normal for guests to arrive an hour or more after the appointed time.

Canberra did have its share of the national pastime of 'Pommie bashing' but I never found it a problem. On the contrary I found that so long as you treated it as a kind of competitive sport you were welcome to engage by bashing back. I found the Aussie no-nonsense directness laced with dry humour both refreshing and infectious. Not long after we arrived there was a campaign to encourage people to eat more local farm produce. ' You're living in sheep country. Eat mutton you bastards,' said the stickers. Difficult to imagine a comparable slogan in the home counties. A sign we saw on a farm outside Canberra said simply 'Trespassers will be composted.' On another occasion we were walking along a fairly remote beach on New South Wales's far south coast. As it was swelteringly hot we felt like a swim. However I had noticed that there was nobody in the water and at the same time spotted a weather-beaten Aussie from an older generation sitting on a log and gazing out to sea. It occurred to me that it might be wise to seek his advice so I asked him if it was okay to swim off the beach. Without hestitation there came the laconic reply 'sure mate, if you want to be part of the food chain.' Only then did I realise that there was a small stream further along flowing into the sea which presumably acted as a magnet for sharks.

As we travelled beyond the artificial confines of Canberra and the Australian Capital Territory (ACT) we came to realise that Australia at that time had developed an ethos of its own for assimilating immigrants. Wherever you came from you were welcome to retain your customs, notably your food, your language and your religion so long as you did not bring the politics of your homeland into Australia. Thus, even though people of Irish descent constitute a significant proportion of the population and have had a major impact in shaping the character of Australia, there was virtually no support for the IRA during its campaign of violence in Northern Ireland. Contrast this with the behaviour at that time of some of the Irish community in the United States.

This ethos seems to owe little to overt government policy but is rather a reflection of strong social and community pressure. Perhaps it is because, unlike the US, Australia is only two or threee generations away from its pioneering days. Whatever the reason Australia seems to make a better fist of integrating immigrant communities than many first world countries including the UK. However there is a rider. In recent years, with the rise of militant Islamism from which Australia's Muslim community is not immune, the government's stance has hardened. Not only is it actively preventing boat people from landing, it is also telling recent immigrants in no uncertain terms that they need to adapt to Australia, not the other way round. We could do with a bit more of the latter approach from the British government together with more emphasis on the responsibilities of immigrants rather than on their rights.

Two months after we arrived in Canberra the Liberal/National party government of Malcolm Fraser was roundly defeated in the elections by the Labor party led by Bob Hawke who portrayed himself as the epitome of the 'ocker Aussie' in contrast to the rather patrician figure of Malcolm Fraser. Although it had close connections with the trade unions, the government was relatively undoctrinaire. It had in Paul Keating an exceptionally able Finance Minister. Among his attributes was a gift for memorable put-downs. Thus on one occasion when the notoriously vain Andrew Peacock was standing for election for the second time as leader of the Liberal party, Paul Keating was asked on a television programme what he thought of Mr Peacock's chances. His memorable reply was that he did not think a souffle could rise twice. Peacock was not re-elected.

When we arrived Australia was just beginning to recover from a serious five year long drought and both morale and the economy had suffered. For probably the first time the dams holding most of Sydney's water supply were down to about 15% of their capacity. The farming community was particularly hard hit and there were prophets of doom proclaiming that Australia should never have been settled in the first place. However, the drought broke soon after the Hawke government won the election. I like to think that my old Irish blackthorn stick, which I waved at the heavens after reaching the top of Mt. Kosciusko, Australia's highest mountain, had something to do with it. The Hawke/Keating team went on to win two more elections and introduced a range of liberalising measures which opened up and transformed Australia's economy.

At the same time there were a number of delicate issues involving states' rights. One particularly serious dispute arose with the state of Tasmania. There the state government had embarked on a major project to build a dam on the Gordon below Franklin river in order to boost the state's energy supply. Unfortunately the site chosen happened to be a UNESCO world heritage site which the Federal Government was bound by international treaty to protect. But when Canberra asked the state government to stop the project Tasmania refused on the grounds that water and energy policy was a matter for the individual states under the provisions of the Australian constitution. Canberra then referred the dispute to the supreme court for a ruling. The court's initial response was to ask for evidence to show how far the project had already progressed.

When Tasmania refused to supply the relevant information to Canberra Gareth Evans, the then Attorney General later to be Foreign Minister, was persuaded by one of his staff that the quickest and easiest way to obtain the evidence would be to ask the RAAF to take aerial photographs of the site. The idea was that they could do this from about 40,000 feet with high resolution cameras and nobody on the ground would notice. However, it so happened that the day after the RAAF was given this task the area was entirely blanketed by low level cloud. Unfazed by this unfavourable weather event the RAAF decided to send in several aircraft to criss cross the target area flying underneath the cloud and so put together a composite photograph of the whole site. As a result even the reputedly dosey Tasmanians woke up to the fact that something strange was going on. They protested vigorously at what they regarded as a totally inappropriate use of the RAAF and a gross infringement of states' rights. Challenged on television to justify his decision Gareth Evans replied with refreshing candour that, as the accused said to the magistrate, 'It seemed like a good idea at the time, your honour.' If only politicians in the UK and elsewhere would follow his example. In the end states' rights had to give way to Australia's international treaty obligations and the wilderness area was saved for the nation and the world. But one could not help sympathising with Tasmania's objection to the misuse of the RAAF.

During this period there was an increasing realisation that Australia was actually much nearer to Asia, which people were beginning to refer to as the 'near north' rather than Europe. Nearer geographically but in other ways too. Immigrants were coming in from south east Asia as well as the sub continent and the Japanese were starting to buy property notably on the Gold Coast. Britain was still the largest overseas investor but increasingly Australia's exports of oil, gas, minerals and livestock were going to China and Japan.

Meanwhile there was a strong tendency in Whitehall to take Australia for granted. After all the great majority of Australians were of British or Irish descent and we therefore understood each other and had common interests and values, did we not ? We even had the same Head of State. So why bother? The flaw in this attitude was that it failed to recognise that, as in a family, so between countries which have close ties, it is necessary to work especially hard to keep the relationship in good shape. Ties of kinship are not enough. Sadly, despite the efforts of the High Commission, we did not have a single visit from a British cabinet minister during my time in Canberra though there were several visits by more junior ministers and by MPs. Happily such political neglect has been remedied since 2010 thanks in large part to the initiative of William Hague There is also now provision for regular high level political and military talks.

This political neglect was, and still is, offset to some extent by the multitude of personal, commercial and financial ties between our two countries, and by the close working relationship between all three armed services, and in the field of defence procurement. At any one time there were scores of British military personnel on various attachments in Australia as well as visits from Royal Navy warships.

Even so the neglect by successive British governments would have mattered more but for the fact that the ties of kinship were, and are, hugely reinforced by our shared monarchy. I believe that the Queen has played a crucial part in preventing our two countries from drifting further apart. During our time in Australia we were struck by the widespread affection and respect for the Queen and the Duke of Edinburgh, and we found little appetite for the notion of Australia becoming a republic. A referendum on whether Australia should ditch the Monarchy and become a republic was lost by a substantial margin.

But the arrangement does have certain practical limitations. Quite apart from the obvious awkwardness of having a non-resident Head of State there is the added difficulty that when the Queen visits a foreign country she normally does so in her capacity as Queen of the United Kingdom rather than as Queen of Australia or any other of her realms. There is also the difficulty that, while Australia can and does receive incoming visits from Heads of State eg the President of the US, such visits cannot be reciprocated through a visit by Australia's Head of State. In practice such technical difficulties have not caused any serious political problem. But I suspect that in the future, as Australia becomes increasingly important in world affairs and after the Queen is no longer with us, there will be a strong movement to establish a republic in Australia with its own Head of State. If and when this does happen I believe that it will be driven by practical considerations rather than by any anti-British sentiment.

As far as the High Commission is concerned one of the consequences of the present arrangement is that on her many visits to Australia it is made quite clear that the Queen is there as Queen of Australia and accordingly the High Commission plays no part in any of the arrangements. The same applies to visits by members of the Royal family.

By the same token when a new British High Commissioner is appointed he cannot very well present his credentials to the host country's Head of State as he would do in a Commonwealth country which is not a realm. Self-evidently the Queen cannot write a letter of introduction to herself. So the solution is that he or she carries a letter of introduction from the Prime Minister of the UK to the Prime Minister of Australia. Now it so happened that when Sir John Leahy arrived to succeed Sir John Mason as High Commissioner the Prime Minister, Bob Hawke, was about to set out on the campaign trail as an election had been called. Somehow I needed to find a way to get Sir John in to see Hawke before the latter left Canberra as it would have been awkward for him to start functioning as HMG's representative before being introduced to the Prime Minister.

Fortunately I was able to arrange with the Prime Minister's Private Secretary for Sir John to meet Mr Hawke at a cricket match between a parliamentary X1, led by Hawke, and the press on the Sunday before he left Canberra. As we arrived at the pavilion we found Hawke already padded up and waiting to go in to bat when the next wicket fell. There was just time for them to meet and for Sir John to hand over his letter of introduction from Margaret Thatcher, which was stuffed into the back pocket of the Private Secretary's flannels for perusal later by the Prime Minister, before Hawke had to go in to bat. It seems to me that this episode illustrates the particularly close nature of the relationship between our two countries. It is hard to imagine it happening anywhere else.

It so happened that after making a breezy 27 runs Hawke's glasses were shattered by a ball which he had attempted to hook. As fragments of glass had gone into his eye he was immediately taken to hospital where they were successfully removed. Apparently the glass shards had miraculously not pierced the eye but simply lay on the surface. Some weeks later at a reception in Canberra I had the temerity to ask Mr Hawke (who by then had won the intervening election) how he had come to be wearing ordinary glass, rather than plastic, lenses for cricket. His characteristic reply, in a reference to his optician, was that in the Soviet Union people were sent to the gulag for much less.

Another example of the close relationship was the decision to mark Australia's two hundredth anniversary by building a sail training ship in Britain, aptly named *Young Endeavour* and sailing her out to Australia in commemoration of the voyage of the First Fleet with a joint crew of young Britons and Australians. The ship was then to be handed over to the Australian government. The idea was conceived in the High Commission though largely financed privately. It fell to Sir Peter Gadsden, the then Lord Mayor of London, to inform Bob Hawke during an official visit of the decision. At first Hawke, who was aware of more elaborate offers from Japan and the US, seemed somewhat underwhelmed. But he was won over when Sir Peter pointed out the gift was meant to be in the nature of a birthday present not an aid programme!

However, despite the closeness of the relationship there could be, as in a family, a good deal of scratchiness from time to time. One particular issue which flared up while we were in Canberra was the perceived failure to clean up the plutonium residue from the nuclear tests which Britain, in concert with the Australian government under Sir Robert Menzies, had carried out deep in the south Australian desert at Maralinga. In fact there were two related issues. One was the damage to health and to the environment from the explosions and from the later botched attempt in the seventies to clean up, which had unintentionally spread the plutonium particles more widely. The other was the claim by a number of British and Australian ex-servicemen who had taken part in the tests that they had suffered permanent damage to their health because of the failure to protect them from radioactive fall-out.

Hawke was lobbied both by aborigines from the area around Maralinga and ex-servicemen demanding compensation. In this situation he resorted to the usual device favoured by governments in both countries when finding themselves in a tight corner. He appointed a Royal Commission to investigate the claims. As the Commission's Chairman he chose a senior judge, the flamboyant 'diamond Jim' McClelland who was well known for his outspoken views on a range of issues. Shortly after Sir John's arrival the judge took exception to some remarks made by the High Commissioner to the press about Maralinga. Initially it seemed as though the judge's reaction could only inflame an already delicate situation. However, the tension was defused when John Leahy telephoned the judge and, after regretting the fact that in this day and age he could not challenge him to a duel, invited him to lunch instead. Eventually, though there were other difficulties along the way, both sides were able to work together constructively. At British expense a more effective clean up of the test sites was carried out.

Back in the 1980s Canberra was still a company town. That is the business of most people there was government or government related, and/or politics and the media. The only other activity of note was in the academic world notably at the outstanding Australian National University. While the politics was often entertaining it could also feel parochial. The repartee and confrontations in the Lower House and in the Senate could be a lot more colourful than at home. But we soon discovered that outside Parliament MPs from all three main parties were happy to mix, mingle and relax on neutral territory. Thus we spent many enjoyable evenings in their company over informal buffet suppers or drinks in our house in Talbot Street.

At the same time we were very conscious that Canberra and the Australian Capital Territory were not typical of Australia and indeed were regarded by many Australians as a highly privileged enclave which they had to pay for. Canberra itself was a compromise which only existed because at the turn of the twentieth century when the Commonwealth of Australia was established neither Sydney nor Melbourne could agree which should be its capital. That the chosen site had developed so attractively around its artificial lake was due in part to the creative genius of the American architect Hugh Burley Griffin.

We heard a number of different theories about the origin of the city's name. The usual explanation is that it comes from an aboriginal word meaning 'meeting place' which would of course be very appropriate. I prefer an alternative version that there used to be in the nineteenth century a cattle station in the area owned by the Campbell family and known therefore as Campbell station. Given their tendency to end every word with a vowel this became known by the local aborigines, who were still in the area at that time, as Campbella station. Either way the name derives from aborigine speak.

Life in Canberra was comfortable, indeed quite seductive, thanks to the climate, the sporting facilities and the company of friends and colleagues. But Val and I were determined to take every opportunity, both professional and on local leave, to explore the real Australia. Thus for example we were able to spend a day with the flying postman out of Broken Hill. This was in a single engined aircraft with a Norwegian pilot, two dogs and a pile of mail bags. We flew over vast stretches of desert at little more than tree-top height between cattle stations each with its own landing strip and accompanying ancient fridge standing proud in the desert with the name of the station painted on the door. This ingenious arrangement provided a safe location for the incoming and outgoing mail for the station which was often several miles away from the landing strip. A good example of re-cycling.

From Broken Hill we hired a car and drove 350 miles on a dirt track road, much of it deep in bull dust, to Tibooburra on the edge of the Sturt Stony desert. During the whole journey we only saw one other vehicle and that was a cross-country motor bike. We caused a bit of a stir when we went into the local pub as, unbeknownst to us, the road from Broken Hill had been closed to non essential traffic for some weeks because of unusually heavy rain which had, as we had noticed, made the road almost impassable in places. However, thanks to years of driving on Tanganyikan dirt roads we were able to get through.

On the way back we had a puncture and found that the spare was not usable. Mercifully it happened only a few minutes away from the only habitation for miles around – a general store run by a remarkable, pioneering couple, Ken and Raylene Ogilvy. Our tyre was shredded but Ken was able to shape a substitute from his collection of old tyres which got us back to Broken Hill. As a result we developed a lifelong friendship with the family.

Many years later, in 2008, we stayed for a few days with Ken and Raylene on the huge cattle station which by then they had created in the middle of the outback about sixty miles from the pub at Cameron's Corner where the borders of South Australia, New South Wales and Queensland meet. Because of the different time zones this must be the only place in the world where New Year can be celebrated three times in one night! Unusually I kept a diary of our safari from which the following is an extract. I include it not least because I am not at all sure for how much longer this pioneering way of life will be able to survive.

Sunday 24 February:

Up early and out and about to soak in the sheer vastness of the red sand landscape all around and the miracle of this tiny oasis created from nothing by Ken and Raylene. They run 2,000 head of prime Hereford cattle, plus a thousand or so Aberdeen Angus on 'ajistment' from Queensland, on one and a quarter-million acres of marginal land which is about half the size of Northern Ireland. To the untutored eye it looks like semi desert. Over the years they have sunk nine boreholes, four of which are now linked to the homestead by a telemetric computer system which makes it possible to monitor them remotely. They have also built several large dams. The boreholes and dams have many miles of plastic pipe running from them to carry pumped or gravity-fed water to a patchwork of cattle troughs. Ken and Raylene have also put in many miles of fencing for mustering paddocks and an extensive network of tracks for their four-wheel drive 'utes'.

Out on the station there are dingos, wild camels and brumbies and of course kangaroos. Rabbits are kept in check by the dingos of which there are many because the station lies to the west of the great dingo fence which runs across Australia from north to south.

It is astonishing to see the superb condition of the cattle reared in this semi-desert country. I have never seen the like anywhere else. They need no supplementary feed, calve on their own, and generally look after themselves as long as they can reach water. They suffer from no pests or diseases and have no parasites. Nor do they have any predators except that occasionally a pack of dingos may attack a calf. In short

Lindon and other stations in the area must be producing the purest, most natural beef on the planet.

During our time in Canberra we were also privileged to be able to visit an aboriginal settlement on a reserve which non-aborigines were not allowed to enter without a permit. The area, several hundred miles north-west of Alice Springs in the middle of nowhere, had been a cattle station before the land was given back to the local aborigines. The previous owners, who surely had a wry sense of humour, had called it Utopia station and the name had stuck. The group we met there were living mainly in the open as their ancestors had done with camp fires and their dogs at night for warmth. They lived on hand-outs from the government for part of each week supplemented by hunting and going walkabout for the rest of the week. I felt sorry for them, caught as they were between two cultures. Our visit also brought home to me the nature of the predicament faced by the Australian government as it tried to integrate the aborigines into the contemporary world without destroying their way of life in the process.

This problem was further illustrated a year or two later when I attended, as a guest of the government, the ceremonial handing over of Ayers Rock by the Governor General, Sir Ninian Stephen, to the aboriginal people. This was to be their special day on which they regained ownership and control of one of their most sacred sites, henceforth to be known by its aboriginal name, Uluru. Accordingly the authorities had decided that it would be appropriate to leave the arrangements in the hands of the tribal elders. These arrangements turned out to be somewhat minimal.

The visiting press and diplomats found themselves corralled in a rope enclosure in the middle of a small clearing in the scrub bush at the foot of the rock. The sun, as usual in central Australia, was blazing hot and there was no shade. The only refreshment was in the form of warm lemon squash scooped in plastic beakers out of plastic dustbins. To make matters worse the planned corroboree failed to materialise and the platform party of tribal elders could not agree on the anthem to be played when the Governor General arrived. Consequently his arrival had to be delayed. When he did arrive he spoke eloquently about the importance of aboriginal culture in Australia. But by then most of his audience were too hot, dusty and tired to pay much attention. More than twenty years later Kevin Rudd made a further attempt to reach out to the aborigines in a memorable public apology for the way they had been treated in the past. Yet more recently the government has rightly banned tourists from climbing Uluru and thus finally recognised its special, spiritual significance for aboriginal people.

Towards the end of our posting we took advantage of a final spell of local leave to fly up to Townsville in northern Queensland at the invitation of Ted Lindsay, the local Member of Parliament who was also a Minister in the Hawke government and with whom we had become good friends. He had helpfully arranged for us to hire a small schooner with a professional skipper on which we were able to sail out to the Great Barrier Reef and then wend our way northwards up to Hinchinbrook Island with a brief interlude on the lonely and lovely island of Orpheus with its exotic inter-tidal coral. We spent one never to be forgotten moonlit night anchored on the barrier reef in a flat calm in the middle of the ocean.

Somewhat less helpfully Ted also took me with him to a mass meeting of burly cane sugar farmers in the town of Ayr. At the last moment he asked me to appear on the stage with him where I was asked to explain why they no longer enjoyed the same access to the UK market as they had before we had chosen to join the Common Market as it then was. I said something to the effect that we were doing our best to reform the Common Agricultural Policy and open up the Common Market to agricultural produce from elsewhere. The audience received this politely although clearly not at all convinced. It may have helped that I also told them that if they were surprised to see me on the platform they were not half as surprised as I was.

At the beginning of 1986 we left Canberra with much reluctance for a home posting. Val had nearly completed a degree in Asian studies at the Australian National University (ANU), and I was much enjoying the many friends we had made and the life style. I had also found that with the High Commissioner away for much of the time in Sydney, Melbourne or elsewhere there was plenty of work for me to do in Canberra. But it was time to move on, and our daughter and her family were in the UK. Val had also somehow persuaded the ANU and Oxford to collaborate so that she could complete her ANU degree under supervision at Oxford. Oxford was the only university in the UK which was able to satisfy the ANU that it could meet their criteria for overseeing the ANU's Asian Studies degree.

Looking back I regret that we in the High Commission were not more successful in persuading HMG to pay more attention to Australia, which is arguably, apart from New Zealand, the country which is closest to us in character, culture, and political orientation notwithstanding its national pastime of pommie bashing. It is also of course an increasingly important bulwark of liberal western democracy in a region where China is becoming ever more dominant. However, in the eighties there was still a lingering sense in Australia of betrayal by the mother country over Britain's perceived failure to protect Australia's economic interests when we joined the Common Market, as it then was, and provide special protection for Australia's traditional exports to the UK. There was also, to put it mildly, not much empathy between Margaret Thatcher and Bob Hawke.

But the world has changed hugely since then and Australia's major markets are now in the Far East, notably China and Japan. I hope that one of the effects of Brexit may be to revive Britain's interest in the Commonwealth and equally the Commonwealth's interest in Britain. Australia has already indicated its interest in concluding an early free-trade agreement with the UK. Meanwhile it is noticeable that Australian news and views feature much more prominently in the UK press and media than a few years ago.

Chapter 10

London Again

B ack in the FCO after seven years abroad, I found myself head of the then Central African Department responsible for relations with the so-called Front Line States which included Zambia, Zimbabwe, Malawi, Mozambique, and Angola. They were all in the front line of the fight against apartheid in South Africa. We also covered the second largest country in Africa, known in those days as Zaire, now the Democratic Republic of the Congo. Our relations with most of these countries were under continuous strain because of Margaret Thatcher's unwavering opposition to sanctions against South Africa. This despite the fact that we were one of the leading aid donors to most of them. So the task was like trying to damp down a fire which is being constantly re-kindled.

Against this background I had much admiration for the then Foreign Secretary, Sir Geoffrey Howe, who took most of the flak and remained calm and unruffled in the face of considerable provocation. At the same time his command of his briefs and attention to detail was comprehensive and impressive. If you had submitted a complex proposal or brief requiring his approval you might well find yourself asked, for example, to explain what you meant by the third sentence in annex D.

I made a number of visits to the region, one of which was with Sir Geoffrey as part of his team. He took a swing through southern Africa to carry out the Prime Minister's wish that he should explain the government's position on sanctions to the leaders of the Front Line States, and persuade them of its merits. This was no easy task, though we had the comfort of an RAF VC10 for the journey. Somewhat surprisingly the worst reception for the mission was in Lusaka where Kenneth Kaunda deliberately kept him waiting for several hours before deigning to see him. There were some who thought that Sir Geoffrey should simply have left but that was not his way.

By contrast Samora Machel in Mozambique could not have been a more courteous host. En route to Maputo Sir Geoffrey, who had done his national service in the King's African Rifles (KAR), asked me if I could think of an appropriate phrase in Swahili which he could use to encourage Machel to stick to the task of rebuilding his country even though it might take a very long time. Something on the lines of 'Rome wasn't built in a day'. Fortunately the Swahili saying *haba na haba hujaza kibaba* (literally, little by little the bucket is filled) came to mind. It seemed just right. It also provides a good illustration of the thoughtfulness and sensitivity with which Sir Geoffrey approached these meetings.

At the meeting itself I well remember Machel describing the problem in South Africa as tribal rather than racial. As he saw it the tribe with all the power happened to be white. Somehow they needed to be persuaded that it was in their own long term interest to share power with the other tribes who happened to be black. It was a vision which only a few years later looked like coming true when Nelson Mandela came to power. Machel's death in a plane crash not long after Sir Geoffrey's visit was a great loss to the region. There were various theories at the time that the plane had been deliberately brought down by the apartheid regime in South Africa which was certainly supplying arms to the Mozambican rebels, Renamo. But the black box recording of the last words of the (Russian) pilots provided ample evidence that in fact they were drunk and had chosen to ignore the on board warnings that they were flying too low and were about to hit the ground.

Margaret Thatcher apparently never forgot the critical part Samora Machel had played in the Lancaster House Agreement on Zimbabwe in 1980 by persuading a reluctant Mugabe to accept it. There is a story that when both Mrs Thatcher and Samora Machel were in Moscow for the funeral of Andropov they happened to meet on the grand staircase in the Kremlin when one was going up and the other coming down. Apparently they stopped half way and warmly embraced, much to the bewilderment of their Soviet hosts.

Apart from the issue of apartheid an underlying theme during my time at CAFD was the on-going Cold War competition between the West and the Soviet Union for influence in the Third World, notably in Africa. This was at its most intense in Angola where Cuba and South Africa were engaged in a fierce proxy war in support of the regime of President Dos Santos on the one hand and the marauding bands of Jonas Savimbi's Unita on the other. At stake were the rich diamond reserves of Angola and its off-shore oil fields.

I had thought that the poverty I had seen in the slums of Old Delhi and Calcutta were as bad as it gets but Luanda was even worse. Nowhere else had I seen raw sewage running down the walls of buildings nor such a complete absence of state or NGO services of any kind. There was also an ominous sense of violence and insecurity. Movement was only safe around the centre of the city and out to the airport. Calls on Ministers were like excursions into some make-believe land of mirrors and dreams. On my several visits I had much sympathy for our tiny staff in the Embassy who were virtually prisoners in their own compound. Their presence in Angola was mainly an expression of hope for the future of a country with the mineral and agricultural resources to become one of the richest in Africa.

Mercifully neither the Soviets nor the Americans had become directly involved in the conflict though the Soviet Union gave material support to Cuba, notably in the form of MiG fighter jets. Eventually it became apparent to both Cuba and South Africa that there was no early end to the conflict in sight. The South Africans in particular were losing too many men and also losing the war in the air because the MiGs were superior to South Africa's elderly Mirages. Thus there was an opportunity for the US to broker talks, brilliantly chaired by Chet Crocker, Assistant Secretary of State for African Affairs, which paved the way for peace and the withdrawal of both Cuban and South African forces from Angola. Eventually this in turn led to the independence of Namibia and contributed to the ending of the apartheid regime in South Africa. Although not directly involved we helped to facilitate the talks which took place in the UK and incidentally provide an object lesson in how effective professional, patient diplomacy can be, especially if it can be carried on away from the spotlight of the media.

As part of the same endeavour to limit Soviet influence in Africa I had proposed that we should offer military training in some basic skills such as first aid, planning and logistics, to officers in the Frelimo army which was battling the Renamo rebellion in Mozambique. This idea was approved by the FCO and by No 10 provided it did not require British servicemen to put their lives at risk by going into Mozambique. Consequently we managed to negotiate an arrangement with Harare for the establishment of a training camp in Eastern Zimbabwe at Nyanga, not far from Mutare and the border with Mozambique. Basic accommodation in thatched huts was built by the Zimbabwean army. I visited the camp in the bush for the first training course run by a very small British army contingent and was greatly impressed by their ability to improvise in a situation where there were few facilities and virtually no teaching aids. I particularly remember a young officer from, as it happened, my old regiment, the Inniskillings. He soon discovered, when trying to teach some first aid, that his pupils had no idea of basic human anatomy. As there were no blackboards he tackled the problem by marking out with white chalk the key organs of the body on the bare black torso of one of the Mozambicans – much to the amusement of the students. I still think that it was absurd that this kind of programme, which arguably made a significant contribution to security in Mozambique, should have had to be paid for from the FCO's tiny budget (similar in size at that time to Hounslow Borough Council) rather than from the far larger aid budget. Security is after all a prerequisite for development.

This kind of project was only possible because at that time Mugabe was still pursuing broadly sound economic policies helped not least by his first wife Sally, a Ghanaian princess. Consequently Zimbabwe was prospering and we had a good working relationship though we deplored the excesses perpetrated against the Ndebele minority. There was always plenty of anti-colonial and anti-white rhetoric but it had not been translated into action and Mugabe himself was still a frequent visitor to Britain.

With the advent of Gorbachev and the beginning of Glasnost and Perestroika, relations with Moscow began to improve somewhat. Consequently it was decided that Tony Reeve, who was the AUS (ie Director) for Africa at the time, and I should visit Moscow for working level talks on Africa at the Soviet Foreign Ministry. As this was when the Thatcherite rush to privatise was at its height Tony made a strong pitch about the merits of privatisation as the way forward for African countries. Instead of the expected counter from the Soviet side on the merits of Communism our interlocutor simply and memorably responded by saying 'It seems that you people are the ideologues now.' This response in itself symbolised the extent to which change was taking place in the Soviet Union.

As part of the same 'great game' of countering Soviet influence in Africa we were also cultivating links with the regime of President Mobutu in Zaire despite its egregious corruption. Accordingly we were developing a modest aid programme there. In that context it fell to me to accompany Lady Chalker on one of her early visits to Africa as Minister of State at the FCO. We spent our three-day visit in and around Kinshasa as it was virtually impossible to travel anywhere else in the country except by air or along the

Congo river. We called on a variety of Ministers and visited various pet projects of President Mobutu then in his heyday. The highlight of the visit, if that is the right word, was a lengthy courtesy call on Mobutu who received us on board his luxury yacht moored on the left bank of the vast Congo river with the lights of Brazzaville just discernible on the distant shore. The call was prolonged not so much because of its content but rather because Mobutu kept disappearing for a few minutes without any explanation and then returning as though nothing had happened. I never discovered whether he was trying to make the point that he had more important things to do or was just suffering from a tummy upset.

During my tenure in the Central African Department I visited all the front line states at least once and met most of their Heads of State and many Ministers and politicians. This was to prove very useful when, after retiring from the FCO, I helped to launch and run the Southern Africa Business Association together with Alistair Boyd, the former Deputy Chief Executive of the CDC. As I have indicated it was never an easy ride because of HMG's continuing opposition to sanctions against South Africa. But thanks in no small measure to the patient efforts of Geoffrey Howe and Lynda Chalker, and to the fact that we were such a substantial aid donor to the region, relations with the countries in the region remained on the whole stable. It is also noteworthy that, despite her stand against sanctions on South Africa and her hostility to the ANC, Margaret Thatcher got on remarkably well at a personal level with many African leaders – not only Samora Machel but also Kaunda, and Hastings Banda of Malawi. She also made a successful visit to the region in 1989 beginning with Zimbabwe.

Chapter 11

Uganda

After nearly four years in London I was offered in the autumn of 1989 the job of High Commissioner in Uganda. Although excited by the prospect, I was also quite apprehensive as I was well aware of Uganda's complex tribal and ethnic mix, and of the fact that the country was just emerging from a long period of violence and turmoil under Amin and subsequently Milton Obote and Tito Okello. But I was much encouraged at the time by the enthusiasm of my predecessor Sir Derek March. It says much about the lastingly negative image the country was given by Idi Amin that our parish rector in Bidborough, when he heard the news of my appointment, asked if we would like the congregation to pray for us.

Val and I arrived in Uganda shortly before Christmas. We had chosen to drive in from Kenya, rather than fly in directly to Entebbe, in order to see something of the country before becoming immersed in the inevitable round of initial calls in Kampala. We were met at the border by David Pearey who had been acting High Commissioner during the interregnum between the departure of Sir Derek and my arrival. David was a great support during our first few months in Uganda and I was truly sorry to see him go the following April on a posting back to London. Our first port of call was with a group of expatriates in Jinja who treated us to a welcome drink of Jinja beer – much better than the ginger beer which we initially thought we were being offered! The drive to Kampala gave us our first glimpse of a green and fertile land. We soon found out that it was also full of charming people many of whom were however still traumatised by the violence and mayhem of the preceding fifteen years.

Although Museveni had come to power in Kampala three years previously it had taken time to overcome resistance in the north and east. Indeed this was still a work in progress. The National Resistance Army, as it was still called at that time, was well disciplined but there were far too many guns in the hands of army deserters from the previous regime and gangs of criminals.

Thus many government, diplomatic and private residences had armed guards for protection. The guards had a habit of firing off a few rounds at random during the night to let would-be burglars know of their presence. We eventually got so used to the background noise of shooting at night that when it gradually died down after a year or so we found the silence much more unnerving and had difficulty getting to sleep.

Although peace had been restored through much of the south and south west these were still early days in Museveni's effort to put the country and its economy back together again after the mayhem and economic free-fall of the preceding years. When Museveni came to power in 1986 Uganda was in the depths of despair. Kampala had come to resemble Beirut at its worst with warring factions in different parts of the city. Law and order had completely broken down, the judiciary and the police force had virtually ceased to exist. Schools and hospitals were neglected and the whole infrastructure of the state was crumbling. In Kampala, even three years on, there were very few shops, no street lighting and the roads were so full of potholes that the joke was that if you saw someone driving in a straight line you knew they must be drunk.

There were still random car hijacks which could easily lead to the driver of the car being killed. As a result we routinely gave three pieces of consular advice to newly arriving expats. The first was to have only one key on your key ring because of the considerable inconvenience of losing all your keys, the second was never look at the hijackers but keep your eyes down, and the third and most important was never fasten your seat belt. There had been at least one death as a result of a driver reaching across to undo his seat belt and thereby causing the hijacker to think that he was going for a gun.

However, alongside the residual trauma and criminal activity, there was a growing sense of hope and optimism about the future in place of the earlier sense of hopelessness and despair. Many of our Ugandan friends told us of how in previous years their main objective had been to stay alive from one day to the next. One of Museveni's Ministers summed up the new mood shortly after we arrived – 'Please tell London that the monsters have gone and they are not coming back.'

Another positive feature of Uganda which we discovered early on is that most Ugandans are refreshingly colour-blind in the sense that it matters not what is the colour of your skin. People you met might either like you, or not, but it was unlikely to have much to do with your skin colour. When we went to All Saints Cathedral just up the hill from our house on the first Sunday after our arrival we soon found the pew where we were sitting filling up from both ends with local people keen to share our prayer book and hymn book as both were in short supply. This was a welcome contrast to our experience in neighbouring Kenya where the pews in which Europeans were sitting were given a wide berth by the local Africans. I believe that the main reason for this difference is that there was never large-scale settlement by white people in Uganda though it was mooted on more than one occasion. Accordingly land was never a serious issue and, partly for this reason, Europeans were not seen as a threat.

One of my first duties was to present my credentials to President Museveni. This was quite an elaborate occasion at State House, Entebbe, a gracious colonial style building with extensive lawns overlooking Lake Victoria which had been the home of successive British Governors. There was a smart guard of honour and the number one band of the NRA which played the respective national anthems. I learned afterwards that the Ugandan anthem 'O Uganda, the land of freedom' had, somewhat ironically, been written by a Brit. Museveni had also assembled most of his senior Ministers to meet me. After I had handed over my letter of credence from the Queen and a personal message from Lynda Chalker, Museveni wished Her Majesty a long and happy reign. This prompted me to wish him the same (he had only been President at that stage for three years). Little did I realise as I did so that over twenty-five years later he would still be there! In a characteristic response Museveni said that he was really a cattle man at heart, and that he would dearly love to retire to his ranch at Rwakitura but was unable to do so because somebody had to run the country. Then, waving in the general direction of his row of Ministers, he added that none of them were up to the job. This cavalier attitude towards his Ministers did not seem to make enemies for Museveni, at least not until much later in his Presidency, partly I suppose because they knew full well not only that he had the support of the army but also that he was highly popular among the majority of the people at that time.

At all events I like to think that from then on I enjoyed a good working relationship with the President whom I was to see frequently, sometimes at my request and sometimes at his. On one occasion we were quietly enjoying our second Christmas day in Kampala when the phone rang in the Residence and Museveni asked if I would come down to Entebbe that morning to see him. Although it was not quite what we had planned I felt it would be both unnecessary and inappropriate to point out that it was Christmas Day. So, as the High Commission was closed and all the drivers were at home with their families, I drove myself and only had with me my Royal Military Police bodyguard of the day, Andy, who happened to be a strapping black British man from Peckham.

When we got to State House we found that all the staff including the protocol people and the President's Private Secretary were also away for Christmas. The main entrance to the house was manned only by Museveni's special NRA guards. As I knew the usual arrangements I went and sat in a side room inside the house waiting to be called to meet the President in a large marquee-type tent on the lawn where he liked to receive his visitors.

Meanwhile, unbeknownst to me, the army guards, seeing Andy sitting alone in the Range Rover, had invited him in and asked him to make himself comfortable in the main reception lounge. As it happened Museveni chose to walk through the lounge on his way to the marquee. With commendable initiative Andy stood up, saluted smartly, and said 'Merry Christmas, Sir'. Whereupon Museveni said ' and who are you ?' I cannot recall what Andy told me he had said in reply but when I eventually came into the marquee by another route, quite unaware of Museveni's encounter with Andy, his first question was to ask who is that African you have with you? I replied 'He is not African, he is British.' Museveni then said 'But he is black' to which I replied 'yes, he is black British' which prompted Museveni to ask 'how can that be?' There followed a lengthy discussion about the necessary conditions for acquiring citizenship from which it appeared that the possibility of obtaining it simply by virtue of birth was an alien concept. I believe this partly explains why Museveni and his government did not feel responsible for the action of many Tutsi Rwandans when, some two years later, they invaded Rwanda from Uganda.

No doubt my ease of access to the President was also due largely to the fact that we were Uganda's number one bilateral aid donor, and to the close relationship which Lynda Chalker had established with him since she had been the first Minister from any western country to visit Uganda after Museveni came to power. On her first visit they had spent several days in discussion at a remote game lodge at Kidepo on the Sudanese border.

Subsequently Lady Chalker made regular visits to Uganda. On each occasion she would bring news of further UK assistance so that she soon became widely and affectionately known as 'Auntie Lynda'. I flatter myself that it also helped a bit that I could still speak tolerable, if somewhat rusty, Swahili from my Tanganyika days. So conversations with the President were often laced with Swahili words or phrases, and I always greeted him in Swahili. On one occasion however he said to me with a chuckle ' High Commissioner, your Swahili is so old fashioned,' which no doubt it was. Swahili's success as a language which is widely understood in eastern and central Africa is partly due to its capacity to adopt and adapt. In Uganda, however, it has suffered from being associated with the language used by the army and by the Tanzanian army when Tanzania invaded Uganda to depose Amin. Thus, although widely understood, it has never become a lingua franca as it is in Tanzania and to a lesser extent in Kenya. There is an apt saying that Swahili was born in Tanganyika, murdered in Kenya and buried in Uganda.

I was, and still am, well aware that I was fortunate to be in Uganda at a time when Museveni was doing many of the right things both politically and economically. Crucially he was willing to listen to reasoned argument, even criticism, provided it was constructive. In particular he was I believe influenced at that time by the views of the exceptionally able Permanent Secretary at the Ministry of Finance, Emmanuel Tumusiime-Mutebile,(ex Balliol) who later became Governor of the Central Bank of Uganda.

I was also fortunate in that we were supporting Uganda's recovery with one of our biggest and most comprehensive aid programmes in Africa. With so much to re-build it was difficult to know what to prioritise. In the event I think we got it about right though of course mistakes were made. One top priority was to help the police to get up and running again by providing both training and equipment, notably Land Rovers and signal sets. We financed the rehabilitation of the police training centre in Kampala and had several senior police officers from the West Midlands Police acting as advisers to the Ugandan police force.

Another priority was to re-build the Judiciary which had been badly demoralised. To lead this work HMG seconded three experienced judges led by Harold Platt who was later knighted for his outstanding work in helping that process and in supporting and encouraging Uganda's own senior judges. Harold was an invaluable source of information and advice for me especially during my first few months in the post. Both he and his wife, Lori, descended from a prominent Austro-Hungarian family, became close friends of ours.

A further key priority was to save and renew the country's generating capacity virtually all of which came from the Owen Falls hydro scheme on the Nile at Jinja. This was originally built while Uganda was still a British Protectorate. It was opened by the Queen just under 50 years after Winston Churchill had prophetically written in his journal of his visit to Uganda in 1908 'what fun to make the mighty Nile plunge through a turbine at this point'. After some thirty years of neglect the dam wall was in danger of collapse and all the turbines needed major repair or replacement. So serious was the cracking of the dam wall's foundations that a consulting engineer on the project said to me that, if the dam had been built to current specifications, it would have collapsed. As it was the Owen Falls project, costing over £30 million, was at the time I believe Britain's biggest aid project in Africa.

To repair the dam wall we had to bring out a team of North Sea divers. As they had to do hard manual work at considerable depth in pitch black water to plug the holes and cracks with concrete blocks they could only stay down for half an hour at a time. Fortunately, because of the strength of the current, there were few crocodiles about! Between stints the divers would sit on the side of the road over the dam stripped to the waist and displaying a variety of colourful tattoos, not to mention the odd ear ring. They were continuously surrounded by an admiring crowd of African kids who had never seen Europeans behave in such a way.

At the same time we had a major programme of support for primary schools and rural health clinics. Both education and health care were in a bad way. Since it was not possible to do everything I think we were right to concentrate on re-building the basics rather than focusing on more prestigious projects such as universities or hospitals though both Makerere University and Mulago hospital badly needed support. One element of the portfolio which I strongly supported was aimed at stimulating economic growth more directly. This included funding to restart textile production at the Nytil factory near Jinja and the repair of a sugar refinery at Kinyara near Masindi in the north. Perhaps the most effective long-term contribution we made was by providing a small number of in-country advisers for key positions in government and through the British Council's programme of scholarships and training in the UK.

As his confidence in our good intentions grew Museveni, while still regarding himself as 'a revolutionary', came to seek our assistance in several unexpected and highly sensitive areas. On one occasion, while I was having lunch with him at his private ranch at Rwakitura, he asked if we could send an experienced Whitehall civil servant for a short time to sort out his private office at State House and streamline the flow of papers which he had to deal with. It is hard to imagine a more sensitive appointment. In the event with the agreement of Sir Geoffrey Howe, we were able to second one of the Private Secretaries from the FCO who stayed for about a month and did an excellent job.

On another occasion when there had been a spate of high profile murders, and the Ugandan police were making heavy weather of finding the perpetrators, Museveni asked me if we could find a suitable senior police officer, preferably from the Metropolitan Police, to take charge of the investigation and report directly to him. When I demurred on the grounds that this was surely a step too far and risked being seen as neocolonialism he responded that this was his problem and I should not worry about it. 'I want to see justice done', he said and added with a twinkle 'whatever happened to Pax Britannica?' So I duly referred Museveni's request to the FCO. This time it was Whitehall's turn to demur. It was clear that there was no longer any appetite to take on such a direct responsibility. Instead we found an experienced Superintendent of Police to come out as a senior adviser. But he had no executive role and was, quite rightly, responsible to the officer commanding the Ugandan police force.

At that time Museveni led a very simple life style when at Rwakitura, in sharp contrast to many of his fellow African heads of state. He had a small ranch house consisting of two adjoining rondavels in the middle of his superb Ankole cattle and a herd of 'exotic', i.e. European, cattle. On my first visit we were rudely interrupted by one of his herdsmen who burst in with no ceremony to tell the President in no uncertain terms that one of the cows was having difficulty calving and Museveni's help was urgently needed. I do not think that the interruption was staged.

Towards the end of my time in Uganda it was decided that we should give an increasing proportion of our bilateral aid in the form of budgetary support direct to the government. The rationale was that this form of aid respects the sovereignty of the recipient state and enables it to take ownership of the assistance while at the same time a degree of accountability to the donor country's taxpayers is provided by attaching a number of conditions. However, the reality is that sovereignty and conditionality are poor bedfellows. In practice it is not possible to ensure genuine accountability without exercising a degree of detailed control of government expenditure which no sovereign country would accept. A further defect is that the more external budgetary support is given the less the host government is dependent on its taxpayers for revenue. This in turn has an obvious negative impact on the democratic process. As somebody has said, 'You cannot build democracy on the back of other people's money.'

Furthermore budgetary support can also cause unintended economic problems especially if it constitutes a significant input into a small economy. For example a substantial injection of liquidity stimulates inflation which can then only be countered by the central bank raising interest rates. This in turn denies local entrepreneurs access to capital at affordable rates. Mainly for these reasons I was uneasy while in Uganda about the then new fashion for budgetary support, and I have become increasingly opposed to it since then except as a temporary measure to help a 'failed state' to get back on its feet.

The task of administering our large and complex aid programme put a considerable strain on the small aid section in the High Commission, ably led at first by Mike Hammond and subsequently by Michael Frost. We also had frequent visits by various experts based at the then ODA's Development Division in Nairobi which covered eastern Africa. These were not always appreciated by our Ugandan hosts as relations at that time between the Ugandan and Kenyan governments were far from easy. Museveni did not get on well with President Moi of Kenya whom he regarded as corrupt. On one occasion, when I had tried to persuade him to be less critical, he replied with more than a hint of exasperation 'but I have borne the cross of Mr Moi for five long years'. A further difficulty was that even with goodwill the extra bureaucratic layer in Nairobi, apart from being expensive to run, tended to complicate and get in the way of dialogue about the aid programme both between the High Commission and the Ugandan government, and between the High Commission and ODA in London.

For these reasons I argued that expert input could have been achieved more effectively and indeed more cheaply by a team of highly mobile officers based in London with the occasional in-country secondment when needed. There were examples of this kind of arrangement working well. For instance ODA had an Energy Adviser, and a Forestry Adviser. Both of them travelled the world to monitor existing projects and advise on new ones. Due to the size of our rehabilitation project at Owen Falls, Chris Leaning,

ODA's Energy Adviser, visited us regularly and there was no need for an intermediary from the Development Division.

A major feature of our aid work in the High Commission at that time was the interface with a multiplicity of NGOs as well as the IMF, the World Bank and the other major donors notably the US, Germany and Denmark. Inevitably there was a certain amount of duplication, not to say confusion, despite the best efforts of successive World Bank representatives to persuade everyone to coordinate their programmes.

From my perspective the best of the international NGOs were Oxfam, Water Aid and Medecins sans Frontières. There were also many Ugandan NGOs, some of which, like TASO (The Aids Support Organisation) founded by the remarkable Noreen Kaleeba to support the sufferers from AIDS and their families, were doing good work on a shoe-string.

We had a number of joint projects with Water Aid as a result of Chris Patten's initiative, when he was the Minister in charge of ODA, to match funding pound for pound for approved projects put forward by reputable NGOs. I formed a high opinion of them. They consistently delivered their projects on time and often below budget. Crucially their modus operandi ensured that the local communities in the rural areas to which they were bringing clean water had ownership of each project, and had measures in place to sustain it before Water Aid undertook it. They did this by consulting the local 'Resistance Council' from the beginning and insisting on certain pre-conditions being met by the community. For example, if the agreed project was to repair an existing borehole, or sink a new one, then the village would be asked to establish a ring-fenced bank account to pay for its maintenance, choose a local villager to be trained by Water Aid to look after it, and set up a small management committee to oversee its proper use. Consequently the project was likely to last. At the time this approach was in marked contrast to many other aid agencies who would conceive, design and implement a project with little or no local participation. Many such projects, in which the local community had no sense of ownership, did not last.

Although there were tensions from time to time there was on the whole a better relationship between the international financial institutions and the Ugandan government than that which existed in many other African countries. In my view this was partly due to the fact that Uganda had the good fortune, as I have previously mentioned, to have an exceptionally able Permanent Secretary at the Ministry of Finance. He was the main interlocutor with the IFIs and consequently there was a constructive dialogue about both the overall shape of development policy and about individual projects. To his credit Museveni had the good sense to allow Tumusiime a fairly free rein as long as he kept the President informed.

While the aid programme provided the backdrop to our relations with Uganda there was much other activity as well including, as Uganda's economy began to revive, in the world of business and investment. Thus we found ourselves increasingly occupied in advising visiting British businessmen on the opportunities opening up, and facilitating their meetings with key Ugandan ministers and officials. Unfortunately increasing prosperity brought with it an increase in 'grand corruption' to use the classic description coined by the late George Moody-Stuart. I did not think then, and still do not believe, that Museveni was corrupt though many of the people around him undoubtedly were. Regrettably the efforts he has made to tackle corruption have not had much success.

Although Museveni continued to regard himself as 'a revolutionary'(his word) and was quite capable of indulging in criticism of the West when it suited him, he also became a fairly frequent visitor to the UK. On one such occasion in 1990 I was summoned back to be present when he called on the Prime Minister, Margaret Thatcher, at No 10. Before leaving Uganda Museveni had warned me that he intended to raise the issue of sanctions against South Africa to which Margaret Thatcher was of course completely opposed. I tried to dissuade him on the grounds that if he did so the meeting was unlikely to be productive. But Museveni insisted that 'it is my duty to raise it.' Accordingly, although I had alerted London to the possibility that Museveni would bring up the sanctions issue, I was more than a little nervous about how the meeting would go if he did. I need not have worried. As soon as Museveni brought the subject up the Prime Minister said very calmly 'Mr President, you know that you will not be able to change my mind and I know that I will not be able to change yours so I suggest that we should just leave it at that and go on to discuss other matters.' With that, honour was satisfied and the rest of the meeting turned out to be both cordial and productive. Among other developments it paved the way for us to send a small military training team to Uganda. Although only six-strong the professionalism of the team clearly impressed their Ugandan counterparts. Also they were able to focus not only on military tactics but more widely on the role of the army in a democracy to act in support of the civil power and within the law of the land.

When Museveni said that he intended to call on the then President Ghadaffi of Libya (who had supplied Museveni with arms when he was fighting a guerilla war in the bush) Mrs Thatcher simply observed that she hoped he would sup with a long spoon. I reflected afterwards that this was not the first time that the Prime Minister had displayed a remarkable capacity for getting on with African leaders despite their widely differing political views.

Throughout our posting I was fortunate to have a well-motivated and capable team at the High Commission both expatriate and locally employed. I should mention in particular my driver Joseph who not only spoke very good English and Swahili but also spoke, or could at least understand, ('hear' as they would say locally) nearly every tribal language in Uganda including Luganda, the language of the dominant Baganda people. His knowledge of the country and its people was invaluable. We also had at the Residence a team of very capable, charming and loyal female domestic staff with whom Val developed a close bond and with whom we are still in touch.

An unusual feature of our life in Uganda was the presence of a rotating six-man RMP Close Protection Unit who provided a constant armed bodyguard for me and initially for Val. They were also tasked to provide a quick reaction force able to reach any High Commission house or flat within five minutes of being called out. As such they provided a vital deterrent as armed break-ins were quite common especially in the first couple of years. Fortunately they were never needed in earnest. There were however several false alarms and the team frequently carried out practice drills. One unintended consequence of their presence was that our much loved German shepherd, Crusoe, who was meant partly to act as a guard dog, always gave a warm welcome to anyone carrying a gun. This was because, without exception, each successive RMP bodyguard treated Crusoe with kindness and made a fuss of him.

Perhaps because he knew that we had a number of specialists in the country including my Defence Adviser, the RMP unit, and a senior police officer attached to the Ugandan police, I had a phone call one day from the President in the middle of a routine meeting in the High Commission. When he came on the line Museveni said without any preamble 'High Commissioner, how long does it take for a hand grenade to explode after you pull out the pin?' Struggling to remember my national service days I said that I thought it was about four seconds. Whether or not that was the correct answer it enabled me to then ask the President why he wanted to know. As a former guerilla fighter himself no doubt he knew the answer perfectly well and in any case could have asked an NRA colleague. He was simply using the question to pave the way for a request for help. It then emerged that the head of the Roman Catholic church in Uganda, Archbishop Wamala, had been taken hostage in his own office beside Rubaga cathedral in Kampala by a deranged individual armed with two hand grenades. He was threatening to blow up the Archbishop and himself unless the government agreed to a number of outrageous demands. In effect Museveni was asking whether we could help to find a way of rescuing the Archbishop without unduly endangering his life or giving in to any of the hostage takers conditions.

In response to Museveni's request I arranged for the DA, our police adviser, who happened to have done a course with the Metropolitan Police in hostage taking, and the Commander of the RMP unit, to join the Ugandan police and security service unit which had surrounded the office where the Archbishop was being held. There followed a tense stand-off which lasted overnight during which our advisers had to restrain the Ugandans from rushing the office with all guns blazing which might well have cost the Archbishop his life.

An almost surreal scenario then developed. First, the Archbishop persuaded his captor to allow him to speak to his secretary on the phone. This enabled him to explain, in Latin no less, what his captor was doing and how he was behaving. He also relayed a request from the captor for food to be brought in by a nun. To this the Ugandans responded by dressing up a female security service officer as a nun and sending her in with a tray of food. She was able to make a mental note of, and report, the layout of the office. Then, as the night wore on and perhaps sensing that his end was nigh, the captor asked to be given Communion by the Archbishop. This prompted the Ugandans to suggest, through the Archbishop's secretary, that they should burst in and shoot the captor while he was kneeling with his back to the door to receive Communion. To his great credit Archbishop Wamala refused to agree to this.

Eventually, as dawn broke, the captor went to the inside toilet to relieve himself. The Archbishop seized his opportunity and rushed out of the office and into the arms of his rescuers much to the relief of all of us. Moments later his unfortunate captor blew himself up. Throughout the whole ordeal the Archbishop demonstrated great courage, coolness and initiative as well as Christian compassion for his captor. The following year he was made a Cardinal. It has always puzzled me how this dramatic episode, widely reported in Uganda, was never, as far as I know, picked up by the press in the UK.

Because of such assets both at the High Commission and the Residence, and the RMP presence, it was possible for me, often accompanied by Val, to travel widely throughout Uganda, unlike most of my diplomatic colleagues. We took full advantage of the opportunity. Consequently I visited almost every district from Kabale in the south west to Moyo and Madi Opei on the Sudanese border, and Kidepo in the north east which could only be reached, other than by air, through wild Karamojong country. Accordingly on one safari we drove there in convoy with our two RMP bodyguards and a police escort. Karamoja is classic African savannah country with wide vistas stretching to far blue horizons. In short very unlike most of Uganda. Despite the earlier depredations of Idi Amin's army there were still large herds of buffalo in the game park, a variety of antelope and some noisy lions whose roaring reverberated round the lodge at night. The Karamojong themselves remained aloof and hostile to outside interference. Significantly their word for 'stranger' and 'enemy' is the same. In recent times they had if anything become more fearsome as they had acquired Kalashnikovs in place of spears to protect their cattle, or from time to time raid the cattle of neighbouring tribes. At one point as we entered Karamoja we passed a group of Karamojong tribesmen with their Kalasnikovs barely concealed from us.

On another safari we drove through West Nile province and via Arua up to the Sudanese border beyond Moyo. En route we passed the rusting hulk of the *Robert Coryndon* lying where she had been left at Butiaba when the port was inundated by an unprecedented rise in the water level of Lake Albert. In her heyday she had regularly carried passengers and cargo across the lake to the then Belgian Congo ports of Kasenji and Mahagi. Crossing the Nile by the only bridge into the province at Pakwach proved to be a rather nail-biting experience as there were still elements of Joseph Kony's Lords Resistance Army in the area and the NRA had mounted a machine gun on the far side of the bridge pointing straight down the road. We had no option other than to drive straight at it hoping that the Union flag on the front of the Land Rover might provide a measure of protection. We had of course no way of communicating with the NRA detachment. In the event we reached their position unharmed and were met by a somewhat inebriated young lieutenant who informed us that he was the 'responding person'. Having satisfied himself that we were indeed properly authorised visitors to the province he waved us on.

I also travelled with Betty Bigombe, at that time a Minister in Museveni's NRM government who, as an Acholi herself, had been put in charge of reconciliation in the north. She did her best to persuade the members of Kony's Lords Resistance Army to take advantage of an amnesty which had been offered by the government and lay down their arms. We stayed in a neat bungalow in the military compound at Gulu. When we arrived the lounge was occupied by a rather large goat which the Minister asked the staff to get rid of. This instruction was taken more literally than she had perhaps intended so that later that evening we had delicious barbecued goat for dinner.

On another occasion I accompanied Otema Allimadi, who had been Prime Minister in Milton Obote's first administration, on a safari up to the Sudanese border when, with the approval of Museveni, he tried to persuade the Acholi to stop any support they might be giving to the LRA. Allimadi had taken refuge in the UK when Obote had been ousted by Amin and had been granted indefinite leave to remain. With considerable difficulty I eventually persuaded the Home Office to give him a written assurance that if he went back to Uganda to help to restore peace in the north he would still be allowed to re-enter the UK.

Kony had inherited from his aunt, Alice Lakwena, the mantle of a resistance organisation in the north based on a mix of magic and pseudo-Christianity. Initially he had attracted some support among the Acholi people because of their hostility to the predominantly southern coalition of tribes under Museveni. But increasingly his campaign came to depend on trying to subdue the local people through brutality and terror. He was, however, never a serious threat to the regime in Kampala. Unfortunately all the attempts to persuade Kony and the LRA to lay down their arms came to naught despite the government's offer of a full amnesty and a resettlement grant to enable them to resume farming. Although several hundred fighters did come out of the bush the main unintended consequence was to cause Kony to intensify his campaign of abducting children to be turned by fear into child soldiers or child wives and prostitutes. Eventually it was a combination of increased pressure by the NRA and stronger resistance by the local people which forced Kony to withdraw first to the southern Sudan and then to the forests of the DRC. Any hope of persuading him to lay down his arms, come out of the bush, and make peace was I believe ended when he was indicted for trial by the International Criminal Court in The Hague.

The RPF Invasion

In October of 1992 there occurred an event which is still controversial today. The self-styled Rwandan Patriotic Front suddenly launched an attack into Rwanda from Uganda. They made some initial progress in the north of the country before they were halted by the Rwandan army with the help of French military advisers, and became bogged down. To understand how this could have happened one needs to appreciate that when Rwanda gained its independence from Belgium in 1959 it was the majority Hutu tribe who came to power. This led to a mass migration into Uganda of the minority Tutsis who had been in a privileged position during Belgian rule. In Uganda they had prospered especially in the south west among their close relatives the Ankole people. But (as previously explained) they were never able to assimilate fully and never lost their common identity. They had, however, been strong supporters of Museveni when he was leading a guerilla war in the bush against the regimes of Obote and finally Tito Okello. Consequently there were large numbers of Tutsis in Museveni's National Resistance Army. They also held a number of senior military positions including, crucially, that of chief of military intelligence.

Thus in my view it is entirely plausible that the two principal instigators of the invasion, Fred Rwigyema (who was later killed) and Paul Kagame, were able to coordinate a plan for Tutsi units in the NRA to gather together with their weapons and cross the border into Rwanda without the specific prior knowledge of Museveni. The attack was planned to coincide with the absence of both Museveni and President Habyarimana of Rwanda at the UN General Assembly in New York. The officer commanding the NRA at that time, General Muntu, told me afterwards that as soon as he heard that groups of Tutsi soldiers had deserted and were moving towards the Rwandan border he had ordered the nearest NRA brigade, which was stationed in the west near the border with the DRC, to try to intercept them. However, according to his account, it so happened that many of the troops in that brigade were Tutsis. Thus, instead of intercepting, they simply joined their fellow Tutsis and crossed the border!

Was Museveni complicit in the invasion plan even if he did not know the details? We may never know for certain. He would certainly have been aware that many Tutsis wanted to return to Rwanda and to see the overthrow of Habyarimana's regime, and he also had much sympathy with them. But he maintained that he was not aware beforehand of the plot to invade and, as far as I am aware, there is no evidence that he did know. Museveni said at a press conference on his return from New York that as soon as he heard of the invasion he informed Habyarimana, who was staying in the same hotel, of what was happening. Nor is it apparent that Museveni or Uganda had much to gain from it. On the contrary the suspicion that Museveni was complicit created problems with all Uganda's donors especially France.

However, it can certainly be argued that once the invasion had started Museveni could have done more to prevent supplies from going through Uganda to the RPF. His defence was that Uganda was not a prison and the Tutsis were not in jail. It was therefore not his business to try to force them to return even if he could have done so. Shortly after the invasion began a visiting French Minister at a meeting with Museveni, at which I was present, criticised the President for letting the Tutsis invade Rwanda. Arguing that they no longer belonged in Rwanda, he inadvisedly commented that after their long sojourn in Uganda they did not even speak French. To this a furious Museveni replied 'Minister, they all speak Kinyrwanda.'

During the year that followed I had several informal meetings with Paul Kagame although at that stage we had not recognised him or the RPF. He made a lasting impression on me as a highly disciplined and determined leader, puritanical in both outlook and behaviour. He was indeed rather like Museveni as he then was though lacking Museveni's charm. It is no surprise that under his admittedly authoritarian leadership Rwanda has become one of the most peaceful and successful countries in Africa. By the time we left Uganda in October '93 there were signs that a compromise peace agreement between the Hutu government of Habyarimana and Kagame's mainly Tutsi RPF, brokered by Tanzania at talks in Arusha, might be on the cards. Tragically, however, it was not to be. Notwithstanding its economic success, Rwanda is still suffering from the trauma of the genocide which ensued after Habyarimana's plane was shot down and the international community failed to intervene to stop the genocide.

On a visit to Kigali many years later with an Eastern Africa Association trade mission we found a well organised and welcoming country clearly benefiting from substantial foreign investment. Kigali itself, nestling attractively among green hills, was well run and prospering. We were told that its remarkably clean streets were due to the President's habit in the early days of personally brushing the street outside his residence on a regular basis and insisting that the ordinary citizens of the town should follow his example. It is no surprise that Rwanda has one of Africa's fastest growing economies and is ranked by the World Bank as one of the easiest countries in Africa in which to do business.

There is however a darker side. As already mentioned the trauma of the genocide of the Tutsis in 1994 has not been exorcised. There are still minor incursions by Hutu rebels across the border in the DRC. There is also tension with Uganda, not least because of a lingering personal antipathy between Kagame and Museveni. Finally the murder or disappearance of several opponents of the regime in recent years suggests that Kagame is becoming increasingly autocratic, intolerant of opposition, and ruthless.

Return towards normality in Uganda

Meanwhile on the domestic front there was a gradual return towards normality. Museveni had launched a major project to develop a new constitution for Uganda which was gathering momentum. This was badly needed as Museveni had wrested power by force in 1986 from the hapless Tito Okello, though with much grass-roots support. Thus a Constitutional Commission was set up to undertake a country-wide consultation exercise with a view to producing a draft constitution for consideration and approval by a specially elected constituent assembly. As a final step the draft constitution, with any amendments which the assembly chose to make, was then to be put to the people in a nation-wide referendum. There can be few countries which have embarked on a more elaborate consultation exercise about a new constitution.

The Commission itself was led by a senior judge, Justice Ben Odoki, and consisted of a number of eminent individuals from various walks of life including the academic world, business, the civil service and the army. Over a period of many months they travelled all over Uganda and collected some 20,000 submissions from schools, trade unions, other civil society organizations and individuals. The British government provided practical support in the form of Land Rovers and computers for the Commission but we carefully refrained from trying to influence the content of the draft constitution.

One of the thorniest issues was whether the constitution should provide for continuation of the one-party system (described in Uganda as a non-party system) or for multi-party democracy. At the time the National Resistance Movement (NRM) did allow for different views in that individuals within the party were free to disagree openly with aspects of party policy and could not be expelled from the party for doing so. Also other parties were allowed to maintain an office. But as they were not allowed to contest elections or even to carry out political campaigns this arrangement was pretty meaningless.

Museveni defended the system on the grounds that Uganda had tried multi-party democracy in the sixties and the result had been disastrous, ending with the army coup led by Amin. He maintained that, in a 'backward' (his word) tribal society like Uganda with only a small middle class with any national consciousness and involvement in national issues, allowing different parties to operate just served to exacerbate ethnic and religious divides. In response I argued that the great defect of his 'non-party' system was that there was no mechanism which allowed the people to bring about a peaceful change of government. Museveni accepted that multi-party democracy was probably the best system for developed societies but maintained that Uganda was not yet ready for it. It is clear that his argument was self-serving but that does not render it invalid especially in the light of Uganda's early post-independence experience. Even with properly functioning and independent civil institutions including the judiciary and a free press it was probably unrealistic to expect our Westminster system to work well in developing African countries with no tradition whatever of a 'loyal opposition'.

Eventually the Commission produced a comprehensive draft constitution. They got round the difficult multi-party issue by inserting alternative sections, one providing for a continuation of the 'non-party'system and the other for a multi-party system. The constitution which was finally adopted by the constituent assembly in 1994 provided for a continuation of the 'non-party' system for five years followed by a mandatory referendum to decide whether to change to multi-party democracy. In due course the referendum was held and approved such a change. Sadly however the change has been more cosmetic than real. As recent Presidential elections have shown the odds have remained heavily stacked against any opposition. Opposition leaders and their supporters have been constantly harassed by the authorities and denied a level playing field. Consequently, and partly due also to the incompetence of successive opposition leaders, Museveni has remained in power long past his sell-by date.

In a bold move Museveni invited the Ugandan Asians, who had been unceremoniously expelled by Amin, to come back and reclaim their property. He saw this, rightly, as a signal to the outside world that the rule of law was being restored and that Uganda was again open for business. In the event only relatively few returned as most had made a successful life for themselves and their families in the UK. Those who did return were mainly the more prominent families, notably the sugar barons and one or two who had owned commercial property in Kampala. Museveni's response to complaints from local Ugandan businessmen was typically robust. He pointed out that they had been exceedingly lucky to benefit from a windfall for twenty years which many had failed to make the most of.

Meanwhile the expatriate community, mainly British, began to expand from the 200 or so hardy souls who had persevered through all the hard times under Amin and subsequently Obote Two and Tito Okello. There was also an influx of aid agencies and international NGOs with their accompanying flotillas of shiny four-by-fours.

Another sign of better times was a resumption of cultural activity by the British Council. The Council had maintained a steady programme of training and scholarships to the UK. The Director of the Council in Uganda, Lloyd Mullen together with his wife Promilla, had always kept an admirably open and hospitable house and had many Ugandan friends. But now the Council decided that it would be safe to resume inward cultural visits from the UK. They chose for the first visit a small group of six black actors from Peckham with a production of Macbeth. I could not help thinking that only the Council could have imagined that Macbeth was the most appropriate play to perform in a country just emerging from years of strife and struggle. After the performance in the National Theatre I took the elderly and gentlemanly Ugandan Minister of Education, Emmanuel Mushega, backstage to introduce the cast to him. The woman starring as Lady Macbeth happened to be unusually tall and stately, and had also shaved all her hair off. When I introduced her Mushega, after congratulating her, said how pleased he was to meet her because when she was on the stage he had not been sure whether she was 'a man or a lady'. To this she retorted in broad cockney 'I'm neither mate, I'm a woman.' Culture and generation shock all in one! At the same performance, at which President Museveni was sitting beside me in the auditorium, Lady Macbeth has the line 'Look like th' innocent flower, but be the serpent under it'. This caused Museveni to mutter 'sound advice from four hundred years ago'.

At the same time, and most importantly, commercial activity and investment interest were also picking up and therefore becoming a more significant element of the work of the High Commission. There was renewed interest from a number of British companies including BAT, Diageo, Barclays Metals and Mitchell Cotts, an old established tea company. The London-based Eastern Africa Association brought in a trade and investment mission. They also helped the Ugandans to organise an investment conference in London led by Museveni. I was particularly pleased when British Airways decided to reinstate a weekly flight to Entebbe via Nairobi after an absence of many years. The first flight in was quite an emotional occasion and for many Ugandans the clearest sign that the country was rejoining the real world.

Even tourism was beginning to revive. The Queen Elizabeth National Park at Mweya was reopened. Likewise tourists could again take a launch trip on the Nile up to Murchison Falls between banks dotted with enormous crocodiles. They had to provide their own accommodation however as the lodge was not operational. Most remarkably the elephants, which had survived being machine gunned by Amin's troops and had fled into the then Zaire, had begun to return to their ancestral home. Most significant for the future of Uganda's tourist industry was the gradual opening up of the home of the mountain gorilla in the Bwindi 'impenetrable forest'. Together with our son-in-law Peter and a close neighbour from Bidborough, we had the rare privilege of being one of the first small groups to be able to find and film a partially habituated gorilla family which included one enormous silverback. The latter did not take kindly to our neighbour standing up quite close to him to get a better photograph and staged a truly frightening display of chest thumping before our neighbour was persuaded by our Ugandan guide to kneel down again.

With the return of peace in most of the country Uganda also began to attract more prominent overseas visitors. Among the first of these was Pope John Paul the Second. His visit lasted for five days and he made a deep impression on all who met him. Val was persuaded with difficulty by the Papal Nuncio not to tell the Pope that he should encourage the use of condoms, at least in marriage, to help in the fight against Aids. However on being introduced to His Holiness along with other Heads of Mission and their wives she somewhat stole his lines by saying 'God bless you'. Shortly before the visit Museveni had been asked on a television programme whether he approved of their use and had replied that, as a former military man, he would not dream of sending his troops into battle without helmets!

Other visitors included Nelson Mandela, not long after his release from Robben Island but not yet President of South Africa, Kenneth Kaunda complete with white handkerchief, and Robert Mugabe. The latter, invited to address a large crowd on the anniversary of independence, delivered a typically strong condemnation of Britain while frequently referring to his audience as 'comrades'. Museveni in response commented that in Uganda it was customary to address people as 'ladies and gentlemen'. I took this as an indication that Museveni was distancing himself from Mugabe's remarks and that the rebuke was intended.

On a lighter note I remember one particular state banquet in honour of the visiting Commissioner for International Development from Brussels when my somewhat eccentric Italian colleague took offence at not being seated at the top table. In protocol terms he probably should have been there because Italy held the Presidency of the EU at the time. However, this was a diplomatic nuance which, not surprisingly, was completely lost on the Ugandans. Unwisely the Ambassador, instead of overlooking the understandable mistake, chose to register a protest by turning his empty plate upside down to indicate that he was not happy with his placement. Unfortunately for him this gesture merely resulted in the Ugandan waiters saying how sorry they were that he was not hungry and accordingly bringing him nothing to eat!

Meanwhile Val, besides running the household with its heavy schedule of entertaining, and maintaining and developing the Residence's large terraced garden, also threw herself into a variety of local charitable activities. These included chairing the Katalemwa Cheshire Home where she helped a number of their physically handicapped children to get access to corrective surgery at Mulago hospital. She also arranged for several of the children to be admitted to the Kampala School for the Physically Handicapped at Mengo. Three of them have subsequently been supported financially right through their schooling by a group of friends in our home village of Bidborough who have also paid for the purchase of a plot of land and the construction of a house for them to live in, and a small shop. Without this support they would probably not have survived. As I write the village is still fund raising for them and for the school in Kampala, led by its excellent Administrator Joy Mwesigwa, which does admirable work among disabled children and is now much bigger than in our day.

Val also became involved with the local Aids Support Organisation (TASO) run by a formidable Ugandan lady, Noreen Kaleeba. At the time, when any form of treatment was in its infancy, the TASO volunteers provided emotional and practical support for Aids sufferers who had nowhere else to turn for help. After relevant training Val became an Aids counsellor and spent much time visiting Aids sufferers in their homes.

Uganda had erroneously acquired an unenviable reputation as the epicentre of Aids in Africa. In point of fact it was no worse than in several other countries on the continent but under Museveni's leadership it had been much more open about the epidemic at a time when others were trying to sweep it under the carpet. Children approaching puberty were warned about the dangers of 'grazing' as promiscuity was called. In sharp contrast with African tradition they would sing songs admonishing their parents and vowing not to follow their bad example. Death notices and obituaries both in churches and in the newspapers often specified the cause of death as Aids.

Drawing on her previous experience as a volunteer prison visitor in the UK, Val also made regular visits to the prison for women in Kampala where most of the inmates were free to talk to her through an interpreter. She also helped to organise numerous fund raising events, both at the Residence and elsewhere, sponsored jointly with other wives in the diplomatic community and prominent Ugandan ladies. These events supported a variety of local and international charities ranging from a hospice run by Mother Teresa's Sisters of Charity to the building and equipping of a special maternity clinic in Kampala.

By way of relaxation we both enjoyed occasional games of tennis which in my case often ended with a delicious plate of smoked goat and a pint of Ugandan beer with Ugandan friends round the pool at the Kampala Club where I was one of the relatively few European members. I was also privileged to be invited, along with my Indian colleague, Niranjan Desai, to join a unique cricket club, the Bagarusi (literally 'old men' in Luganda). The Club had been founded in the fifties by the then Governor of Uganda, Sir Andrew Cohen. The necessary qualifications for membership were that you had to be over 40 years of age or over 40 inches round the waist, or preferably both. Consequently both Niranjan and I spent many a happy Saturday or Sunday afternoon playing cricket both in Kampala and further afield in Uganda. In the process I like to think that we both played a small part in re-establishing the game throughout the country partly by making gifts of cricket equipment to needy clubs and individuals.

During my last year in the country the Uganda Cricket Association hosted a tour by the Cavaliers, a mix of professional and amateur cricketers from England which was inspired and organised by Michael Wingfield Digby. Such was its success that it led to a reciprocal visit to England the following year by a Ugandan side who played a series of matches against teams such as the Royal Navy and the Guards, most of which they won. The only match they nearly lost was the one which I had arranged against Bidborough, probably the only time in the history of cricket when a village side has played against a country. The reason for the unexpected draw was that Bidborough, unbeknownst to me, had strengthened the side by bringing in one or two ringers. Meanwhile I had suggested to the Ugandans that they should take the opportunity of a village match to relax and let some of the youngsters who had travelled with them have a game. I should not have been so naive!

Another favourite recreation when time allowed was fishing for Nile perch in Lake Victoria. Back then they were plentiful and some of them were enormous. On more than one occasion we came back from 'the supermarket' as we called it with a fish large enough to feed most of the patients in Nsambya hospital in Kampala. Val set the record with a Nile perch which weighed in at 38 kilos.

During the first two difficult years in particular we came to regard Kenya as our local leave destination – a kind of R and R resort. It also helped that we still had friends there from our Tanganyika days. On one occasion we travelled with them far into Samburu country in northern Kenya. There we had dinner with Wilfred Thesiger who had made his home among the Samburu people. Sadly by then he had become a rather angry old man lamenting the damage done by the arrival of the motor car to the lifestyle of proud people like the Samburu or the Marsh Arabs. Goodness knows what he would have made of the internet. We and the High Commission staff were also fortunate in those early years in being able to truck in most of our provisions from the NAAFI shop in Nairobi.

Eventually on my 60th birthday it was time to pack our bags and leave. I did so reluctantly and with a feeling of much unfinished business. But I have many happy memories of Kampala and Uganda. Among them are the honking of Egyptian geese as they flew in over our bedroom every morning as though to say that it was time to get up, the taste of young goat steamed under banana leaves, and the sight of delicate papyrus fronds waving gently against a deep blue sky. Most all I remember the warmth, sense of humour and fun of the people, and their resilience in the face of hardship. We could learn from them.

In retrospect I believe those years in the early nineties were Museveni's best. Politically he put together an administration in which tribal and religious interests were carefully balanced. By imposing strict discipline he made sure that the army, though the dominant force in the country, behaved reasonably well towards the civilian population. This was in marked contrast to its predecessors under Amin and the second Obote administration. Although he is himself an Ankole from western Uganda he treated the influential Baganda tribe, who dominate central Uganda, with respect and allowed them special privileges. The Lukiko, the Parliament of the Baganda, was restored though with limited powers. In 1993 he allowed the Kabaka (King of the Baganda), who had already been invited back from exile, to be crowned, or rather 'coronated', as they say in Uganda. At the time I had my doubts about the wisdom of this gesture especially when I saw Museveni seated below the King during the coronation ceremony and heard the Kabaka take an oath to defend his kingdom against all enemies. However, despite some tensions, Museveni's gesture does not seem to have been as politically destabilising as I had feared.

Sadly it is Museveni's reluctance to allow himself to be replaced through a fair and open democratic process, and his evident determination to remain in power for as long as possible and perhaps found a dynasty of his own which is the main concern now, together with the rampant corruption which he has failed to control. Consequently the remarkable achievements of his early years in power are increasingly forgotten as the older generation who benefited from them passes on. They should not be. Not only did he restore peace and law and order to most of the country, but he also rescued the economy from free fall with the help of the IMF, the World Bank and the donors, not least the UK. Above all he gave back hope and optimism to a people who were in the depths of despair.

Chapter 12

New Horizons

We returned to the UK in October 1993 and spent some time settling in to our home in Bidborough, and considering what to do next. Alistair Boyd, who had just retired at about the same time as Deputy Chief Executive of CDC, suggested that we should start up a new business association covering all the SADC countries in southern Africa. There had been previous trade associations which had collapsed, so there was a vacuum. Furthermore, South Africa had just emerged under Nelson Mandela from the shadow of apartheid and was in the process of rejoining the real world. For these reasons his suggestion seemed like a good idea and I readily agreed. At about the same time I was invited to become a part-time external lecturer at the School of Oriental and African Studies (SOAS) on their 'hands on' General Diplomatic Studies (GDS) course ably designed and run by Dr Peter Slinn, ex-FCO Legal Department.

Somewhat to my surprise I found both occupations much more fun than I had expected. Alistair and I launched the Southern Africa Business Association (SABA) in the summer of '95 at a meeting in CDC with a guarantee of support from 40 founder members. With a considerable amount of pro-bono assistance from a variety of companies with interests in the region, including Clifford Chance and KPMG, the membership grew rapidly to well over 100 ranging from some of the biggest companies on the London Stock Exchange to small consultancies. They also spanned nearly every business sector from mining to manufacturing to transport and construction, to agriculture and of course the service industries including banking. Only the oil companies stood aloof. Somewhat surprisingly the SMEs, which arguably had the most to gain and certainly had the least to pay, were sometimes the most reluctant to join.

The key to success in the early days was the generous offer by Sir Keith Stuart, then Chairman of Associated British Ports, of the free use of an office and office facilities in their Headquarters in High Holborn for an initial period of three months. Once we were up and running we were able to move to Sir John Lyon House on the Embankment which had been the venue for the regular auctions of the tea trade. Later on we were fortunate enough to be able to rent space in Queensland House in the Strand, courtesy of the Agent General for Queensland. We shared the fourth floor with the Australia and New Zealand Chamber of Commerce UK. It possibly helped that some of our members had connections in Australia and that I also still had contacts there and was an active supporter of the Britain Australia Society. I was also lucky to have a succession of very capable PAs.

One of the pleasures of the job was the opportunity to travel widely in southern Africa where I still knew a number of former colleagues in the various High Commissions and Embassies. Thanks to their help, and later with the help of local SABA representatives, I was able to call on a range of ministers and senior officials up to and including Heads of State, as well as a wide range of business people and organizations. During my six-and-a-half years in the job I visited every country in the region, with the sole exception of Lesotho, some of them several times. Val usually came with me and acted as hostess on numerous occasion as well as unofficial (and unpaid) driver.

Of the countries in the region where I like to think that we were able to add value for our members at that time, Zimbabwe was the most interesting both politically and commercially. Consequently I went there more often than anywhere else during the nineties. I had several meetings with President Mugabe while he was still pursuing a reasonably rational economic policy. This was of course before his arbitrary seizure of the white-owned farms. On one occasion I was talking to the President in the margins of an international investment conference in Harare in which we were both participating. As I recall it we were discussing the government's emphasis on the need for rapid indigenisation of senior positions. At the request of some of SABA's members I said that several of the President's Ministers were talking to companies off the record and telling them that if they wanted to continue doing business in Zimbabwe they would also need to share part of the equity of the company with specific individuals. I pointed out that this kind of threat was damaging to investor confidence in Zimbabwe. Although presumably he knew perfectly well what was happening, this was not something which Mugabe wished to hear within possible earshot of other people. At this point he seized my hand in a tight grip clearly intended both to shut me up and to make it look as though we were the best of friends. Either way it was a clever ploy.

In the late 90s Mugabe was still a fairly frequent visitor to London. On one of his visits I arranged a small luncheon for him with some of SABA's key members. At this time he could still be very charming and apparently welcoming of foreign investment even though he still indulged in anti British rhetoric from time to time. We also still had the British military training team in Zimbabwe, to which I have referred in a previous chapter, which he seemed to appreciate. 'You British are so addictive,' as he once said.

However, his attitude towards Britain changed after a stormy meeting with the then Minister for Overseas Development, Clare Short, soon after new Labour came to power in 1997. Apparently he had asked her why Britain was not honouring the Lancaster House provision that it would pay compensation to white farmers whose land was requisitioned for local African farmers. She is reported to have replied that the provisions of the Lancaster House Agreement had nothing to do with the incoming government. A strange reply given that the Agreement had the status of an international treaty. Mugabe was furious. Ironically there was a team from the UK in Zimbabwe trying to agree the arrangements under which such compensation could be paid. Not surprisingly they were however having difficulty in agreeing with the Zimbabweans the criteria for selecting the local farmers.

After that, with the death of his first wife Sally and his subsequent marriage to Grace, things went from bad to worse and I did not see Mugabe again. I believe that he always had a ruthless streak as he showed with the persecution of the Matabele in the eighties. But it seems that Sally had been a restraining influence for many years. After she had gone, and he had also seen that he was losing support in the country, he launched the policy of arbitrary eviction of the white farmers as a way of regaining the support of the veterans of the independence struggle in particular and of the people more generally. After years of harassing the opposition led by Morgan Tsvangirai it seemed for a while that the story could have a good, if not a happy, ending with the establishment of the Government of National Unity. However it was not to be and in the end Mugabe has left Zimbabwe a sad and impoverished country. It could have been so different.

While Zimbabwe and of course South Africa were the most beautiful of the countries I visited, Namibia was the most spectacular with its unique flora and fauna. We had one especially memorable journey on a dirt road over the hills from Windhoek to Swakopmund on the coast. On one occasion we were looking for a single welwichia plant which survives in the desert from one year to the next with virtually no water. A helpful Afrikaner suggested we should follow the track for about five kilometres. We would then see 'a half track' on the right and a few hundred metres beyond we would see the welwichia on the left. We were wondering how on earth we would recognise half a track when suddenly we came upon it. It turned out to be a perfectly preserved armoured vehicle from the first world war with a combination of wheels and a caterpillar track and with a scattering of empty ammunition boxes around it. The small encampment was clearly a relic of the South African invasion of the then German colony of South West Africa. It had been perfectly preserved by the dry air of the desert.

Swakopmund itself had something of the look and atmosphere of a Bavarian village dropped into Africa. On the outskirts of town, on the side of the road leading to the port of Walvis Bay stands an ancient steam locomotive on a plinth with the words 'Hier stehe Ich. Ich kann nicht weiter'; an amusing take on Martin Luther's famous statement from the pulpit nearly five hundred years ago which started the Reformation. However, on the plinth it refers to the story of the engine which for many years had hauled imported timber for construction on a narrow gauge railway from Walvis Bay to Swakopmund until eventually it could go no further.

On the Sunday of our visit we decided to attend the Lutheran church in the centre of town. To our surprise all of the congregation were European. When we asked where the Africans were we were told in no uncertain terms that this was a church for Europeans and the Africans had their own church in another place. We found this anachronistic echo of apartheid both repugnant and full of foreboding for the future of racial harmony in Namibia.

Apart from regular reports on political and economic developments and investment opportunities in the various countries, SABA's other main functions were to provide a ready-made network of contacts for the members, and to lobby both the British government and governments in the region on issues of concern to the members. This also included engaging in dialogue with the aid and trade directorates of the European Commission in Brussels and suggesting input into Commission policy papers. This activity was usually carried on in conjunction with our sister business associations in the UK, the

West African Business Association and the Eastern Africa Association, and sometimes as part of the European Business Council for Africa and the Mediterranean (EBCAM) based in Brussels. In the process I found that the Commission had some very able people working for it but they were often hamstrung by political and bureaucratic constraints. Consequently to an even greater extent than in most bureaucracies the default position when dealing with a perceived problem was to write another paper about it rather than to take any appropriate action. I also learned that the best and most useful contacts were not necessarily those in senior positions.

EBCAM itself is a unique organisation of business associations based in Europe with a focus on trading with, and investing in, Africa. Two of the key participants are the Afrika Verein in Hamburg and CIAN in Paris. There are several other member associations, not least the Belgian- Luxembourg Chamber of Commerce in Brussels which provides the secretariat and an office for EBCAM. In order to simplify the UK's representation in EBCAM we created an umbrella body, The British African Business Association(BABA). Although it claims to represent some 2,000 companies EBCAM punches well below its weight both with the Commission and with European and African governments. This is partly a consequence of its very loose structure and partly because the interests of its members do not necessrily coincide. Nevertheless it provides a potentially useful network of contacts and can help to open doors for visiting trade missions to African countries.

Mirroring the EU, EBCAM also has a rotating presidency which used to change annually. During my time as Chairman of BABA an important feature of the year was the annual plenary meeting when the presidential baton changed hands. It was the responsibility of the association which would hold the presidency of EBCAM for the following year to organise the meeting and surrounding events. Usually the event was held in the capital of the host association or in another prestigious location. Apart from the meeting itself there was usually a two-day programme of events and visits both for the delegates and their spouses, and there was considerable competition between the member associations to outdo each other

It so happened that the year before it came to our turn our Italian colleagues in Assafrica had arranged a splendid event in and around Rome. So in the following year the spotlight was on the Brits to see what we could do. Thanks to the help of a former FCO colleague, Andrew Carter, who had become Warden of St George's House in the grounds of Windsor Castle, we were able to arrange both the plenary meeting, a dinner which included a number of Ambassadors and High Commissioners, accommodation for the EBCAM delegates and their wives, all within the Castle grounds, and a visit to the State Apartments in the Castle itself. Judging by the reaction of our guests honour was satisfied. The event also sat comfortably within the objectives of St George's House.

I always hoped that we could find a way to merge the three UK-based business organizations into one, despite their very different origins and character. Sadly however that has not proved possible. At one stage we in SABA had come very close to agreeing a merger with the Eastern Africa Association.

At the same time I continued my lectures at SOAS focused on the practice of diplomacy at the coal face rather than international relations theory. I was given considerable help by the FCO's Training Department which provided me with a number of practical, problem solving exercises based on real life scenarios. The lectures included such subjects as policy analysis, negotiation, drafting and bilateral and multilateral diplomacy. The General Diplomatic Studies course was always over- subscribed with up to 80 post graduate students from a wide range of countries both in the developed and the developing world. Most came from the Middle East and east Asia notably Singapore, Malaysia, Hong Kong, and Japan. Some also came from Europe especially Sweden and Ireland, from the United States and Canada and from Africa. Many were actual or potential young diplomats. Others were already employed in the professions or by international companies.

Although they were very able and articulate I was sometimes surprised at how far removed from the practice of diplomacy in the real world were the theories of some of my academic colleagues. However the interface with the students was fascinating. In the process I probably learned more from the students than they ever did from me. One memorable achievement, if that is the right word, of one of the courses was bringing together an Israeli and a Palestinian student who were subsequently married.

During the past few years I became increasingly involved with the Overseas Service Pensioners' Association, as a Council member and latterly as Chairman of the Council. The Association, which was founded in 1960, represented the former members of Her Majesty's Overseas Civil Service (previously the Colonial Service). Initially the focus was on protecting the pension arrangements of the members. More recently however it shifted to protecting the good name of the Service through providing first-hand accounts of what British colonial administration was really like in the years leading up to independence and to countering the more ill-informed criticisms of British colonialism in the media and the academic world. This was done partly through the OSPA Journal, partly through a series of seminars on different aspects of colonial rule held in conjunction with London University's Institute of Commonwealth Studies led by Professor Philip Murphy, and partly through letters to the press and the BBC. In particular it was made clear through eye witness testimony from former practitioners that the main purpose of administration was about the practical business of development and preparing the various colonies and protectorates for independence. It was certainly not about perpetuating Empire. The picture contrasts sharply with the negative, and indeed often grotesque, image painted by many British and US academics with no first-hand knowledge. These ideas have gone unchallenged for far too long.

Some of the participants in the seminars were from the colonies themselves. Unfortunately it was not possible to cover the Indian subcontinent in this way, mainly because of anno domini and partly because India had been administered from the nineteenth century by the Indian Civil Service, a totally separate and unique service. There was however one notable exception, Surendra Nihal Singh, who was old enough to have experienced the Raj as a student. I had first made his acquaintance in Delhi when he was Editor of the *Indian Express* and we had remained in touch over the years. When I asked him if he had really had any first hand contact with the Raj, his memorable reply was 'well I did dance with Pamela Mountbatten, would that do?' As secretary of the Delhi University student union he had invited Lady Mountbatten to open a new student hall and she had accepted. Some time later he was invited to a ball given by the Viceroy and hence the story. At that particular seminar, on the legacy of empire, we were privileged to have my old boss, the late Lord Carrington, as our keynote speaker. While chatting to him over a coffee break I cheekily asked him what he was now doing. With a twinkle he said that he was working on a book about all the famous people he had known and what they were really like. It would however only be published after he was dead. We shall see.

We also had many memorable contributions from elderly but still remarkably spry ex HMOCS officers and spouses. One redoubtable lady of almost 100, who had been the wife of an administrative officer in the then Sudan, told how they often went on tour by train as there were more railways than roads. At night it was sometimes too hot to sleep in the carriage so they would bed down on the platform of the wayside station where they had stopped for the night. On such occasions the advice was to to 'keep your elbows well in' because of the danger from passing hyenas.

Regrettably we had to close the OSPA down at the end of 2017 because too many members were dying or becoming infirm and, by definition, could not be replaced. At closure the average age of the remaining members was over 90. But the Council were determined that there should be a memorable farewell celebration. We should go out with a bang. Consequently we arranged a formal reception and lunch at the Grand Connaught Rooms in London in June 2017. To our surprise the event was attended by over 400 members and friends from around the world. Its success was greatly enhanced by the presence at the reception of HRH The Prince of Wales as Guest of Honour. He went out of his way to meet many of the guests and also gave an entertaining and inspiring address. It was an honour and a privilege to welcome everyone and to be able to introduce His Royal Highness to members who had served in so many countries around the world. As we left the Connaught Rooms in the late afternoon I had a strong feeling that my little wheel of time had gone full circle.

In her farewell reflections on the Overseas Service Pensioners' Association the Deputy Secretary General of the Commonwealth, Dr Josephine Ojiambo, said 'Whilst we bid farewell to the OSPA, its work and its legacy will live on'. I am pleased that we have been able in several ways to ensure that the legacy does live on and is accessible for future generations. The joint seminars mentioned above were recorded verbatim and published. Secondly, the Bodleian Library in Oxford has taken possession of all the OSPA Journals (published twice annually since 1960) and its key records. They will be made available for academics and researchers. Thirdly, material from OSPA members is being collected and included for publication online through the website www.britishempire.co.uk which is run by Stephen Luscombe. Dr Valentin Seidler of the University of Vienna has recorded interviews with OSPA members for inclusion in a digital archive for future academic research. Bristol City Museum is accepting material from OSPA members to add to its existing collections based on the former British Empire and Commonwealth Museum. Finally, thanks to the efforts of the man who was OSPA's outstanding Secretary and Editor of the Journal for many years, David Le Breton, there is now an expanded entry in Wikipedia which provides a brief history of the Colonial Service, later Her Majesty's Overseas Civil Service, and of OSPA.

I believe that over time this legacy will contribute to a more balanced analysis of the unique achievements of the Empire, not least during the period of transition from Empire to Commonwealth. In particular it should help to remove the slur which is sometimes cast on the servants of that Empire both British and, just as importantly, local.

Chapter 13

Reflections

Looking back now over a long and varied, not to say chequered, career I feel blessed to have had more than my fair share of good fortune. My first incarnation as a district officer in Tanganyika gave me a unique and privileged insight into the world of rural East Africa, and left me with a great admiration for the resilience and good humour of its people. It also left me fascinated by the flexibility and subtleties of Swahili.

I have more mixed feelings about the ICI years. Although hierarchical, the company ethos was highly supportive of staff both through its generous terms of employment and through its unique joint consultation mechanism. There were many delightful colleagues and I learned much about how a major international company operates. It was a very comfortable life. Yet somehow I never really felt that I fully belonged. The three years in Malaysia were certainly the most interesting and enjoyable. I feel that the full story of the long and sad demise of ICI, often described as the bellwether of British industry, remains to be written.

My twenty-three years in the Diplomatic Service was the best of times. On the whole morale was high, we were confident and had a clear sense of purpose. Most colleagues were fun to work with and we had a succession of Secretaries of State whom we respected. Towards the end of my career in the Service Information technology was beginning to nudge in but it had not yet taken over people's work, and indeed their lives, to the detriment of both. Nor was it considered necessary, as it evidently is now, for a diplomat's work to be carried out in the full glare of publicity. This makes it that much harder to negotiate quietly and effectively to the benefit of both sides. The Brexit negotiations are a graphic example of this problem.

One other reflection is I believe worth recording. Like other colleagues in the Diplomatic Service I had the privilege of working with members of the intelligence services and of seeing some of their reports if they were relevant to my area of responsibility. Like our own diplomatic reporting much of the intelligence proved to be sound and reliable, but not all of it. Despite the various Whitehall arrangements to analyse these reports, there was unfortunately, and probably still is, a tendency among some Ministers to treat all such reports as true and reliable because of their provenance, their often sexy 'top secret' classification, and other caveats. The problem is compounded if there is no diplomatic reporting with which they can be compared, as was the case for example in Iraq where we had no Embassy in 2003 at the time of the Iraq war.

At least since the often quoted Elizabethan aphorism that an Ambassador is 'an honest man sent to lie abroad for the good of his country' it has been widely thought that diplomats cannot be trusted to tell the truth. Strange as it may seem in an era of 'false news', I can only say that I do not recall any occasion when I had instructions to lie or distort the truth, though there were a few occasions when it was necessary to be 'economical with the truth' to quote Lord Robert Armstrong. I was also lucky in that I cannot recall ever having had to carry out instructions about a particular policy with which I fundamentally disagreed, though I often disagreed over the detailed implementation of our aid policy. Fortunately Suez was well before my time!

As we led our busy, nomadic existence around the world Val and I had the great privilege of meeting and mixing with a wide range of interesting people in all walks of life. At the same time we had the opportunity to visit many fascinating and beautiful places before they were swamped by mass tourism. It was often hard work and there were many challenges, not least for our children who had to put up with a very disjointed childhood. Rather like a vicar in a parish, a diplomat, and indeed his or her spouse, on an overseas posting are on duty seven days a week. Even when relaxing over a game of tennis or over a beer, so long as they are in their host country they will be seen as representing their home country and government. Nevertheless I would not have wanted to do anything else for those twenty-three years. Eventually we settled down in the small village of Bidborough in a beautiful part of West Kent and soon discovered that we had been lucky enough to find ourselves in a vibrant community where neighbours and friends still look out for, and help, each other.

As it happens I also had the somewhat unusual experience in those days of seeing from the inside both the worlds of business and of government. It was a time which saw both the twilight of Empire and the transformation of Britain from a major player on the world stage to a medium-sized country still adapting to its changed status. With the controversy over our membership of the EU behind us I hope that the coming years will see an enhanced role for the Commonwealth.

Appendix A

Office of the Prime Minister,
P.O.Box 9000,
Dar es Salaam.

CMC 17/65/049

1st May 1961.

Dear Cullimore,

I feel I should write to you personally at this time when you and numbers of your colleagues may feel that you must make decisions about your future.

Some Administrative Officers have, I know, already decided to leave Tanganyika, and to them I would say thank you for what you have done and good luck in whatever you decide to do.

To those of you who are undecided, the first thing I want to make clear is that my Government, and therefore the great bulk of the people of Tanganyika whom we represent, are really in need of your help; and we will be for a long time to come. I have said so on many occasions, both in Legislative Council and outside. So have several of my colleagues, although their references to you do not always get as well publicised as one or two speeches which are contrary to Government's policy and which do harm to Tanganyika. Anyway, let it be clearly understood that such wild remarks as were recently reported as having been made by Mr.Mwanjisi in Cairo do not reflect my views or my Government's or those of the vast majority of the people of this country. You can account for them by the heady atmosphere in which they were delivered; and so I hope you will ignore them. At all events, let me repeat here that it is not only technical officers we wish to retain. We need our experienced administrators, our corps d'elite as the Governor called you the other day, because it is they who keep the whole machinery of Government working.

I did not feel I could write to you in this personal fashion until we, as a Government, could see that you were being properly treated materially. Now that the Flemming award has been made and the compensation scheme is in being, I feel entitled to ask you to stay and help us. That is not to say that I think you will have no difficulties. I know many of you will have serious worries about education, although we have done what we can to help you there with the allowances that make it easier for you to educate your children in your own country. Some of you may feel, though I believe you are wrong, that medical and other services may deteriorate; or that there will be less companionship with people of your own background on out-stations.

I do not brush these worries aside as though they do not matter, but I want to appeal to the sense of mission which our Administrative Officers have always felt. It is your sense of mission which has seen you through the challenges of the past. I can offer you challenges too and I don't think they are so very different from the challenges that brought you out here. Together

- 2 -

we have still got to make something of Tanganyika that we can
all be proud of; and surely that is enough of a challenge for
anyone in a continent where so much ill-feeling and unhappiness
abound.

So I am not suggesting that from now on no irresponsible
statements are going to be made by junior politicians in this
country.   Such a suggestion would be silly.   What I am seriously
suggesting is that you should not be put off from your great task
by such statements and by such irresponsibility.   I am not
suggesting that you will have no trials and difficulties and
frustrations in the future.   I am suggesting that the difficulties
alone should not head you off from playing a part in this country
where the chances of constructing a genuine community of goodwill
are stronger than anywhere else in Africa.

It is my duty to appeal, as I have done above, to your
sense of duty towards Tanganyika.   But perhaps you will feel that
it is not my business to appeal to your patriotism towards your
own country.   Nevertheless, I want to do so, because I feel so
strongly that British interests and the interests of Tanganyika
are the same in this regard.   All the leaders of British political
life and all the leaders of this young emergent country are
remarkably united in their desire to see Tanganyika off to a good
start and in their views as to how this can best be done.   Would
not Britain's interests be damaged as well as Tanganyika's if you
and your colleagues left us in such numbers that the fabric of
government could not be properly maintained?   Could you feel happy,
if you had left us for any but the most strong and compelling reasons,
if we then proceeded to make a mess of our trust here because we had
not enough British administrators to help us?

And so I am asking you to stay with us if you possibly
can.   Stay with us and help in a job which will, I am sure, be as
full and as varied and as challenging as anything you have done
hitherto.   If you can stay indefinitely, that is what I would like
best - subject only to our Africanisation policies, and I have said
before that we are so desperately short of trained Africans that
these policies are unlikely to affect you adversely for a good time
to come.   If you cannot stay indefinitely, then I would ask you
most seriously to consider whether you cannot stay for the next two
or three years with us, for it is those years, above all, which will
be our testing time.

I attach to this letter a note from my Permanent
Secretary, which, in the light of plans already announced, indicates
the kind of openings for which I need you.   I hope you may consider
where you can best fit into the pattern and let your Provincial
Commissioner know.

Yours sincerely,

Julius K. Nyerere.
(Julius K. Nyerere)

Appendix B

The Development Set

Excuse me, friends, I must catch my jet –
I'm off to join the Development Set;
My bags are packed, and I've had all my shots,
I have travellers' cheques and pills for the trots.

The Development Set is bright and noble,
Our thoughts are deep and our vision global;
Although we move with the better classes,
Our thoughts are always with the masses.

In Sheraton hotels in scattered nations,
We damn multinational corporations;
Injustice seems easy to protest,
In such seething hotbeds of social rest.

We discuss malnutrition over steaks
And plan hunger tanks during coffee breaks/
Whether Asian floods or African drought,
We face each issue with an open mouth.

We bring in consultants whose cirmcumlocution
Raises difficulties for every solution –
Thus guarenteeing continued good eating
By showing the need for another meeting.

The language of the Development Set,
Stretches the English alphabet;
We use swell words like 'epigenetic'
'Micro', 'Macro', and 'logarithmetic'.

Development Set homes are extremely chic,
Full of carvings, curios and draped with batik.
Eye-level photographs subtly assure
That your host is at home with the rich and the poor.

Enough of these verses – on with the mission!
Our task is as broad as the human condition!
Just pray to God the biblical promise is true:
The poor ye shall always have with you.

Ross Coggins

Index